11/15

D0718881

Pr
at

Books should be returned or renewed by the last date above. Renew by phone **03000 41 31 31** or online *www.kent.gov.uk/libs*

Libraries Registration & Archives

CUSTOMER SERVICE EXCELLENCE

CSE

Kent County Council kent.gov.uk

speaking. Whether you're daunted by who is in the audience or just want to find ways to make your stories more engaging, this book is packed full of practical tips and wise insights to give your speeches and presentations the wow factor.'

Graham Allcott, author of *How to be a Productivity Ninja*

'A must-read for every TEDx speaker preparing for their inspiring talk. Practical, insightful and easy to read, with valuable tips on how to become a confident and authentic public speaker. Simply brilliant!'

Lynn Tabl

C333842058

'In my 20 years as a professional public speaker, I have never come across a more effective or authentic guidebook as *How to be Brilliant at Public Speaking*. Not only did I pick up invaluable tips on how to improve my own performance, when I shared this material with my teenager, she read it from cover to cover to "up her game" in public debate. Whether a novice or seasoned pro, this book has the power to allow anyone who reads it to captivate and hold an audience in the palm of their hand.'

Dr Mary Helen Hensley, chiropractor, metaphysical healer, motivational speaker and Simon and Schuster's author of *Promised by Heaven*

'Sarah's book is a blueprint on how to gain your voice and deliver a great speech, time after time. Packed with useful tips and practical steps, it will help you to perform with creditability and believability. A book that you will keep coming back too!'

Sue Terpilowski OBE, Director of Image Line Communications, London Policy Chairman of the Federation of Small Businesses, speaker, lobbyist and panellist

How to be
Brilliant at
Public Speaking

PEARSON

At Pearson, we believe in learning – all kinds of learning for all kinds of people. Whether it's at home, in the classroom or in the workplace, learning is the key to improving our life chances.

That's why we're working with leading authors to bring you the latest thinking and best practices, so you can get better at the things that are important to you. You can learn on the page or on the move, and with content that's always crafted to help you understand quickly and apply what you've learned.

If you want to upgrade your personal skills or accelerate your career, become a more effective leader or more powerful communicator, discover new opportunities or simply find more inspiration, we can help you make progress in your work and life.

Pearson is the world's leading learning company. Our portfolio includes the Financial Times and our education business, Pearson International.

Every day our work helps learning flourish, and wherever learning flourishes, so do people.

To learn more, please visit us at **www.pearson.com/uk**

How to be Brilliant at Public Speaking

Learn the six qualities of an inspiring speaker – step by step

SECOND EDITION

SARAH LLOYD-HUGHES

PEARSON

Harlow, England • London • New York • Boston • San Francisco • Toronto • Sydney • Auckland • Singapore • Hong Kong
Tokyo • Seoul • Taipei • New Delhi • Cape Town • São Paulo • Mexico City • Madrid • Amsterdam • Munich • Paris • Milan

PEARSON EDUCATION LIMITED
Edinburgh Gate
Harlow CM20 2JE
Tel: +44 (0)1279 623623
Fax: +44 (0)1279 431059
Website: www.pearson.com/uk

First published 2011 (print and electronic)
Second edition published 2015 (print and electronic)

© Sarah Lloyd-Hughes 2011, 2015 (print and electronic)

The right of Sarah Lloyd-Hughes to be identified as author of this work has been asserted by her in accordance with the Copyright, Designs and Patents Act 1988.

Pearson Education is not responsible for the content of third-party internet sites.

ISBN: 978-1-292-08796-2 (print)
       978-1-292-08798-6 (PDF)
       978-1-292-08797-9 (eText)
       978-1-292-08799-3 (ePub)

British Library Cataloguing-in-Publication Data
A catalogue record for this book is available from the British Library

Library of Congress Cataloging-in-Publication Data
Lloyd-Hughes, Sarah.
  How to be brilliant at public speaking : learn the six qualities of an inspiring speaker - step by step / Sarah Lloyd-Hughes. — Second edition.
    pages cm
  Includes index.
  ISBN 978-1-292-08796-2
  1. Public speaking. I. Title.
  PN4129.15.L65 2015
  808.5'1—dc23
                        2015023186

The print publication is protected by copyright. Prior to any prohibited reproduction, storage in a retrieval system, distribution or transmission in any form or by any means, electronic, mechanical, recording or otherwise, permission should be obtained from the publisher or, where applicable, a licence permitting restricted copying in the United Kingdom should be obtained from the Copyright Licensing Agency Ltd, Saffron House, 6–10 Kirby Street, London EC1N 8TS.

The ePublication is protected by copyright and must not be copied, reproduced, transferred, distributed, leased, licensed or publicly performed or used in any way except as specifically permitted in writing by the publishers, as allowed under the terms and conditions under which it was purchased, or as strictly permitted by applicable copyright law. Any unauthorised distribution or use of this text may be a direct infringement of the author's and the publisher's rights and those responsible may be liable in law accordingly.

All trademarks used herein are the property of their respective owners. The use of any trademark in this text does not vest in the author or publisher any trademark ownership rights in such trademarks, nor does the use of such trademarks imply any affiliation with or endorsement of this book by such owners.

10 9 8 7 6 5 4 3 2 1
19 18 17 16 15

Cartoon illustrations by Sarah Lloyd-Hughes
Cover design by Two Associates

Print edition typeset in 10/12pt ITC Giovanni by 71
Print edition printed and bound in Great Britain by Henry Ling Ltd, at the Dorset Press, Dorchester, Dorset

NOTE THAT ANY PAGE CROSS REFERENCES REFER TO THE PRINT EDITION

Contents

Part 3 Balance

Understand which content makes the most powerful talk

Part 4 Freshness

Public speaking your audience will remember for ever

Part 5 Fearlessness

Stepping boldly beyond your comfort zone to make your speaking sizzle

Part 6 Authenticity

Returning to the core of you that's naturally inspiring

About the author

Sarah Lloyd-Hughes is a popular speaker on confidence and inspiration, a multiple award-winning coach and social entrepreneur, and founder of Ginger Training & Coaching.

Featured in the TEDx series of public speeches, Sarah is an energetic, original and deeply authentic speaker who works with professionals and entrepreneurs to help them communicate with courage. She has successfully taught thousands of people across multiple continents. As a speaker on confidence, Sarah teaches that the best way to inspire is by being yourself.

Sarah's award-winning Ginger Team now run practical and high-impact public speaking courses, based on the content of this book. With trips to London's Speakers' Corner and a live 'Gala Finale', the *Inspiring Speakers Programme* is the practical way to take on the *six qualities of an inspiring speaker*.

A Coaches Training Institute (CTI) trained co-active coach and practising Buddhist, Sarah suffers from a life-long obsession with the hunt for the full potential of human beings – a theme which weaves itself enthusiastically through her work.

Deep inside, Sarah is really a frustrated artist. As consolation, she adds a personal touch to her books, speaking and training by illustrating them with her unique and slightly ridiculous 'doodles'.

For more information about Sarah's work, please visit www.gingerpublicspeaking.com.

Acknowledgements

For those who dare to have a voice

Writing about inspiring public speaking is a constant challenge and reminder to practise what you preach. I have no better examples in this than my fantastic Ginger training team who challenge themselves and me to go deeper and further with our collective impact. Rona, Nicky, Bev, Lukasz and those still to come – you bring the Ginger magic to life.

My work would be nothing without the people who are willing to step forward and say, 'Yes, I'd like to be an inspiring speaker.' To my programme graduates and brave current clients, thank you for your courage. You are bringing fearless change to the world around you.

To my noble Buddhist teachers, my ongoing gratitude. Anything sensible in this book originated with you.

To those who risk your lives for freedom of speech, you are an enduring inspiration. Thank you and please keep up your hard work.

As ever, I must thank my family and husband Lukasz for being the constant foundation of support from which I can leap. My confidence to do this starts with you.

To you the reader, may these words benefit you and those who hear your voice.

The six qualities of an inspiring speaker

What this book will teach you

- Public speaking is an *act of leadership:* we can bring change and impact through the spoken word.
- Inspiring public speaking comes from *being yourself:* authentic speaking is *infinitely* more powerful than copying someone else's technique.
- Confident public speaking is not about *ditching the nerves,* it's about *embracing them:* nerves are energy that brings power to your speaking.
- Great public speaking is not about *getting it right:* mistakes are the cracks that add personality and charm to your speaking.
- To learn to inspire others, adopt the *six qualities of an inspiring speaker:* rather than sticking behaviours onto your personality, this approach helps you find the inspirational qualities that are already inside you.

Imagine you've just finished an important piece of public speaking. It went better than you could have ever dreamed. Your audience are beaming at you and you know that you hit the nail on the head. Everyone in the room leaves feeling more knowledgeable, inspired and ready for action.

This is closer to reality than you might think. By absorbing the six qualities of an inspiring speaker featured in this book, you too can engage and inspire an audience.

Yet if you feel anything like I did when I first started speaking, it will seem like miles off. I remember watching those 'natural born public speakers' – people who just appear to leap up on stage and spontaneously say the right thing to wow everyone.

It seemed to me like they had a magic gene that allowed them to razzle dazzle their audience with their intelligence, humour and charm. And then when I thought of myself speaking, I felt as though I was surrounded by neon lights telling everyone just how terrified I was.

It's easy to believe that you're the only one who's ever felt intimidated by public speaking. It's easy to focus on all those speakers who seem effortlessly to impress. And it's easy to silently protest, 'But I don't have anything to say', or 'Why would anyone listen to me?' or 'I just can't do it!' But you're not the first – or the last – public speaker to have those worries.

Beyond all proportion, public speaking is quoted as one of the most feared activities in the modern world. As American comedian Jerry Seinfeld famously quipped, 'to the average person, if you go to a funeral, you're better off in the casket than doing the eulogy'.

Although we hold on to the myth that in public speaking you either 'have it or you don't', there's really *no such thing as a natural born public speaker* – just as there's no such thing as a natural born judo master, chess champion, accountant or any other expert.

The secret is that those 'naturally masterful' speakers have put in an enormous amount of time and positive effort to get where they are. They started where you are and they've battled their own fears, they've scratched their heads about what to say and they've pushed themselves beyond what they thought possible. The results can knock the socks off an audience.

So there's no reason why you can't do the same.

In fact, anyone who can carry on a conversation can be a brilliant public speaker. How can I be so sure? First, because I've coached thousands of speakers and I've given up trying to guess who will turn into the best speakers. I've seen shy introverts step onto the stage and blow everyone away with powerful words and I've seen bouncy extroverts mumble and splutter until nobody in the audience is left listening. Public speaking is not about your personality, it's a skill that we can all learn.

Second, I know anyone can learn to be a brilliant public speaker because I've come through it myself. I feared public speaking my whole early adult life – and like most *sensible* people adopted a 100% avoidance strategy. I was happy avoiding the spotlight, until one day I was offered the chance to win my dream job. I *really* wanted that job. All I had to do was deliver a series of short speeches. *Timed* speeches. To 200 people at a conference.

Gulp.

I vividly remember standing outside that conference room with sweaty palms, dry throat and jelly legs. Every part of me felt awkward, even my hair. I repeated my opening line to myself again and again, desperately hoping to remember it. Yet as my autopilot switched on and I found myself walking through the crowd and to the stage, I had no idea whether a single word would come out.

From those beginnings, people now say these sorts of things about my speaking:

Sarah is outstanding on stage. She's riotously fun, totally engaging, experienced and inspiring.

Inspiring, passionate – watching Sarah in action is an affirming and empowering experience.

Sarah is a fantastic presenter and teacher. Watch her, learn from her and your public speaking will benefit.

How is such a difference possible if good speakers are born rather than created?

It wasn't that (distinctly average) speech that revolutionised my public speaking, although I *did* get the job. The experience fired up my love of speaking and I badly wanted to be better. I watched hundreds of speakers and eagerly studied what made them powerful. I saw that some speakers could *just about get through it*, but that I didn't feel moved by them and I didn't remember them afterwards.

Then I saw that some speakers do more than *just about get through it*. They inspire. That's what I wanted to learn. And the secrets of these inspiring speakers are what I want to share with you in this book.

Before I could learn about inspiring speaking I had to unpack some commonly held public speaking myths.

The myth of the public speaking rule book

My early attempts to become an inspiring speaker led me to take training – as you do. There are plenty of excellent speakers you can pay good money to learn from and they will inevitably share their anecdotes about what has worked for them and present them as a fact – *'Copy me and you'll be a successful speaker.'* I tried.

I learned where to put my hands, when to step forward, when to move to this 'anchor spot' on the ground. I learned when to deliver a buzz phrase and when to *close the sale.* But all this was making me feel more nervous rather than more natural because all the time I was being told to be someone else, rather than embracing my own personality.

Learning from the 'public speaking rule book' is the standard approach in training and while it works for some people, it didn't work for me.

Those speakers I saw taking this route looked professional on the outside, but they weren't the ones who inspired me. The speakers who inspired me were spontaneous and full of character. They connected with the audience, they brought life and depth into the room. And they were very different to each other in terms of their body language, their personality and the structure of their talks. They had developed their own unique and inspiring style.

The myth of 'getting through it'

Sitting in the back third of a conference one day, I noticed that some speakers grab the audience and lead them somewhere, while others seem just to be getting through it to fill time before they sit down again.

Reflecting on my own speaking, I realised I was the second type of speaker. I was so nervous about getting through my public speaking that I thought it was a success if I simply survived it. I couldn't have been more wrong!

Succeeding in public speaking means creating change in the audience.

A crucial revelation came upon me – that *public speaking is an act of leadership*. Audiences look to the speaker for influence. They want the speaker to impact how they feel. They want to be led on a journey.

What they don't want is for a speaker to just get through their talk without creating change.

The myth of beating the nerves

My next wish as an aspiring inspiring speaker was to do away with the nerves. I interviewed tens of my favourite speakers to figure out how they got over their nerves. But the answer that came back was resounding. 'I still have nerves,' they told me, 'I've just learned how to channel them into something useful.' These speakers had somehow learned to embrace the nerves, to be comfortable in their own discomfort, rather than running away from their fears.

Indeed, they're not alone. Some of the world's greatest speakers have expressed huge anxieties about speaking. Gandhi as a young lawyer in South Africa professed to being terrified of standing up in court. Churchill had a stutter as a young man and would obsess for days about every speech. What brought these speakers to the level of inspiring others was that they didn't let their nerves stop them.

The myth of making mistakes

The biggest shock for me came when I realised that these inspiring speakers also make mistakes sometimes. And that I even love them because of those mistakes. I had imagined that public speaking was all about knowing your lines, yet suddenly I realised I couldn't be more wrong.

Whenever I stuck to script I thought I did a good job, but my audience never quite connected to my message. Then one day at an important gig my shoe got caught in the stage and I couldn't help bursting into laughter. My audience followed suit and everything relaxed. All of a sudden I'd connected with my audience and I couldn't just go back to the over-rehearsed script in my mind. Instead I spoke like a human being. It was probably the most inspiring speech I had ever given.

People are inspiring

When it comes down to it, there's something fundamentally inspiring about each and every one of us as human beings. In that sense there's absolutely no difference between you and Martin Luther King Jr. While you may not have his audience, or his moment in history, there's no reason why you shouldn't be as good as him at public speaking – or better. You naturally possess the six public speaking qualities I will focus on in this book, even if you currently aren't able to use them in public speaking situations. With an injection of technique and some fearless practice, you will learn that there is nothing stopping you from being a brilliant, inspiring speaker.

The six qualities of an inspiring speaker

The most inspiring public speakers, then, are united not by what they physically do on stage but by the underlying *qualities* they display. By understanding and mastering all six qualities, you too will become a powerful, inspiring speaker.

Adopting these qualities is a six-month process I take speakers on, which involves plenty of practice and feedback. So as you continue through this book, please complement your intellectual learning with public speaking practice and feedback.

The Public Speaking House has three pillars, which relate to the content of your speaking, and three layers, which relate to you as a speaker. Each of these will form a part in this book.

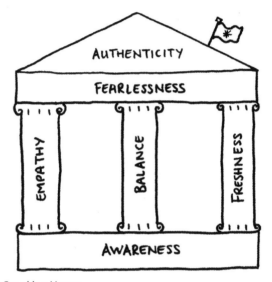

The Public Speaking House

The three layers of you, the inspiring speaker

Awareness: most rookie speakers enter autopilot and lose control of their actions. Awareness of your body, your voice and your nervous habits gives you the space to choose how to behave rather than being at the mercy of adrenaline.

Fearlessness: this is about going beyond your comfort zone to benefit your audience and your message. It is about learning what habits restrict your speaking power and bravely stepping beyond them.

Authenticity: this is the ability to be true to yourself when other people happen to be looking. This is the most simple yet the toughest of all the six qualities – and the key to truly powerful speaking.

The three pillars of inspiring content

Empathy: the best speakers know their audience intimately and shape what they say around this insight. The empathy pillar shows you how to improve your public speaking by focusing on the needs of your audience, forgetting about your nerves in the process.

Balance: like many of the greatest movies and plays, the best speeches have one clear concept and take their audience on a compelling journey. Balance is the sensitivity to know what information goes where to convince and excite an audience.

Freshness: this is about thinking creatively to provide a memorable experience for your audience. Forget about 'death by PowerPoint' and learn to create innovative and exciting public speaking.

And it works!

This book is not just based on abstract theory, it's grounded in methods that really work. Speakers who have followed these methods find that they're improving beyond their highest expectations.

Mike, a senior manager at an insurance company, hated public speaking so much he almost quit his job when he was asked to present at a company conference. Luckily he didn't and by investigating the six qualities of an inspiring speaker, he realised that he too had the power to inspire. Today he is an impressive and confident public speaker – and he even admits to enjoying it.

Journalist Elliot used to 'plan the flu' whenever he was asked to speak at a conference or event. In spite of his exceptional knowledge, he felt that if he tried to speak about it in public he'd be found out as an 'impostor'. Through using these methods, Elliot built his confidence, won an award for his public speaking – and has promised to embrace whatever public speaking challenges he's offered.

Finance worker Yasuko found it terrifying to communicate with her Western clients, especially because her culture encouraged humble and subtle communication. She would rather hide than stick out. After learning about the six qualities of an inspiring speaker, she delivered a masterful, passionate and funny speech to a live audience in England.

They are not alone. Countless speakers who have followed these methods have benefited from:

- **Greater confidence in all manner of communication situations:** if you can display more confidence in public speaking, your interviews, team meetings, sales meetings and even one-to-ones will follow suit.
- **Better career prospects:** when you can speak well, you'll find that you're the one who's asked to represent your team, project or organisation. Studies show that the more visible you are, the more opportunities head your way.
- **Business success:** entrepreneurs and small business owners find that speaking with power helps them spread the word about their company. A company with a strong, authentic figurehead attracts business.
- **Greater self-expression:** this work goes way beyond public speaking. We ask you to use public speaking as a tool for creating change in the world around you. This is big work that encourages you to consider yourself a leader.

If all of this sounds too far for now, don't worry – this book will also give you all the basics to tackle nerves and 'get through' a piece of public speaking. Just don't be surprised if you start to inspire.

Chapter

1

Key wisdom from this chapter

- **Authenticity wins:** audiences are increasingly looking for speakers they trust – and showing you're a genuine human being is the best way to win them over.

- **Speaking from the heart is not just 'fluff' – it works:** if a speaker engages the emotions of an audience, they are more able to influence them.

- **With authenticity comes power:** knowing that you're being authentic gives you unshakeable solidity in your public speaking.

- **Purpose beats nerves:** when you have a purpose behind your speaking, it becomes more important than any nerves you might be feeling.

It starts with authenticity

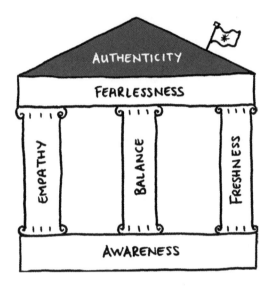

The first and last quality of an inspiring speaker that we'll investigate is authenticity. This is the roof of the Public Speaking House – the place of maximum power that we're trying to get to. Authenticity is, by nature, already a part of you, so it's both a destination and a place to start.

Be natural

I've often heard the concern from aspiring public speakers that standing up in front of an audience to speak can feel fake. When we see motivational speakers, politicians and salespeople using public speaking techniques to manipulate, exaggerate, twist and even falsify information, it's easy to see why.

Authenticity means being natural when other people happen to be looking. As we'll see in Part 1, this isn't always as easy as it sounds, as public speaking can feel anything but natural. We habitually put up barriers. Powerful (and sometimes uncomfortable) clothing, 101 academically verified facts and even a 'public speaking voice' are all ways we try to prove to our audience we are worthy of the stage, yet perversely they can be exactly what switches the audience off.

When a speaker is honest, unpretentious and frank we judge them less harshly, we listen harder and for longer, and we feel more inspired by what they have to say.

Speak from your heart

I strongly believe, as do so many of today's top professional speakers, that great public speaking comes from the heart, not from the head. As neuroscientist Antonio Damasio has shown in his work, decision-making is guided by emotions. Even if we think we're very logical, we are in fact persuaded primarily by feelings. Much more than good technique and a solid structure, then, talking from the heart is an important tool for creating connective and persuasive public speaking.

Speaking from the heart may sound 'fluffy', but it's really very practical. It means communicating from your passion and your humanity, rather than primarily from your logic or your defence mechanisms.

Look at the appeal of TED Talks, where speakers are *encouraged* to speak from the heart, versus politicians who seem to be taught the opposite. Who do you trust more? Whose speeches do you want to listen to? Audiences are turning away from the bright lights of slick rhetoric and impossible promises towards humble, genuine and emotional public speaking experiences. Indeed, we've always gravitated towards the *real* personalities, from Gandhi to Jamie Oliver.

And it's not just speakers with a grand mission – every day in business you see authentic speakers winning over their audience, from the onstage power of Facebook COO Sheryl Sandberg to the humble charm of Sir Richard Branson, through to the passionate team leader in a meeting room.

Speakers who cannot access their authenticity – from politicians, to teachers, to business leaders, to activists – risk switching their audiences off.

The case of Phineas Gage

Phineas Gage was a railroad construction foreman in 19th-century America. In 1848 an accident left him with a metal rod through his skull, damaging his pre-frontal lobe. Incredibly Gage survived the accident with no lasting side effects, other than severe difficulties in decision-making. Antonio Damasio's analysis of this and other similar patients shows a connection between decision-making and emotional centres of the brain. The conclusion: emotions help us to make decisions. This means that the public speaker who uses emotion will be more persuasive.

What is perfect authenticity?

The authentic you is the real you, who's always with you wherever you go. It comes out whenever you're relaxed, whether you're spurring on a colleague to do better, having a rant about your big passion, or giving kind words to a loved one.

So what does authenticity mean?

1. Your message and your behaviours match

When a speaker says one thing and does another we quickly mistrust them. Likewise when a speaker is saying the right sort of thing to impress but their body language tells the audience they're not sure about their message, we see it. As Prime Minister, Gordon Brown was often shown to have incongruent, inauthentic body language. Yet when he stuck up for the 'No' vote in the Scottish Independence Referendum in 2014, you could see that he believed in his message. That made him powerful.

2. Honest interaction, human to human

As TED speaker Brené Brown once said,[1] 'Vulnerability is the *first* thing people wish to see in others – and the *last* thing we wish to show of ourselves.' While we're taught that showing our emotions is a sign of weakness, in public speaking it's a sign of strength, even in the business world.

3. Having a deep purpose that guides your speaking

We all see things in the world we'd like to change, whether we'd like to inspire more eco-friendly toilets at the office or eradicate global poverty. By becoming aware of a deeper purpose behind our speaking, we crank up its power. Renowned speakers like Churchill, Martin Luther King Jr and Emmeline Pankhurst each harboured a sense of purpose in their public speaking that went far beyond themselves.

If your speaking has no purpose and your fear is big, you will show only a little of your personal power. If you have a personal purpose, like badly wanting to get a job or win a contract, you'll come across with more power, but the fear still may be bigger.

But if you have a beyond personal purpose your fears become secondary. Now you will use every aspect of your personality and every fibre in your body to bring about change.

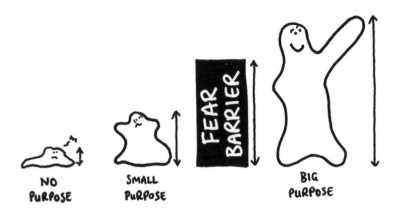

| NO PURPOSE | SMALL PURPOSE | BIG PURPOSE |

4. Having a sense of certainty that's independent of anyone else

As we'll see in Part 5, a powerful speaker doesn't need to seek the approval of someone else; they hold an inner confidence that comes from an authentic purpose. Truly authentic speakers can say the tough truth, even at risk of being unpopular.

Find your authentic power

Finding your authentic power is a life-long quest, rather than a 15-minute exercise. But you can start your quest by asking yourself two sets of questions.

1. What's my personal purpose?

Ask yourself:

- How will I benefit from public speaking?
- What opportunities and possibilities does it deliver to me?
- What excites me about speaking?
- What will I miss out on if I avoid speaking?

While personal purpose is not enough, it's an important starting point. I would never have become a public speaker unless I had understood my personal purpose – I was simply too scared of it. The only reason I faced my fear of public speaking was because I realised my dream job was more important to me. Knowing what I wanted, I was able to stand up and authentically say, 'This is who I am and what I have to offer. I want the job and I know I can do it.'

2. What's my beyond personal purpose?

To access all of your power, your message should serve a wider purpose than just yourself. Ask yourself:

- What is my message? What change am I trying to create by speaking?
- What is important about my message to the wider world?
- What value does it bring to my audience?
- If I *don't* speak, who will *never* benefit from my message?

If you're a campaigner or inspirational speaker, your purpose may be obvious. But what if you're just delivering a 'mundane' message, or don't quite know what you stand for?

Every speaker, whatever the topic, has the opportunity to link their words with something deeper or more inspiring. An accountant might speak because she's helping people move closer to their dream lifestyle. A consultant might speak because he lives for the spark of excitement on his clients' faces. You just have to look deeper: what's important about your weekly team meeting? What was the original purpose behind this lecture? The answers to these questions are the source of your passion for your subject – and your reason to stand up and be heard.

Keep your authentic reasons for speaking in mind as we progress through the next chapters.

Part **1**

Every speaker has a mouth:
An arrangement rather neat.
Sometimes it's filled with wisdom.
Sometimes it's filled with feet.

Robert Orben

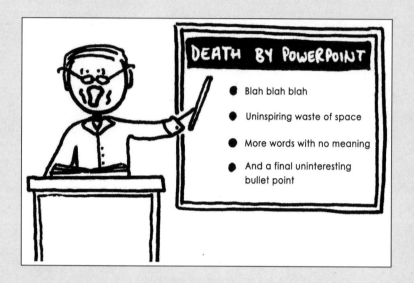

As he clicked through to his 'Thank you' slide, Edgar Mumble looked up at his bored audience. 'Phew, it's over,' he thought with relief. 'That was much longer than I imagined.'

'Erm . . . any questions?' he muttered to the first row, scratching at a red patch on his neck. His offer was met with silence. Edgar collected his books and scuttled out of the room to a thin ripple of applause.

'That went well,' he said to himself. 'I'll do the same presentation again next year.'

Awareness

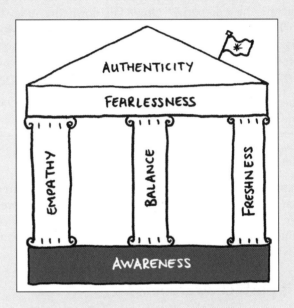

In Part 1:

- Key causes of fear and how to overcome them.

- How to use your body to make your nervous system feel safe.

- Indications of nerves in your body language and vocal delivery.

- How to choose the impact of your body language and vocal range – for bringing credibility, energy or connection into your talk.

A traveller walks along a pathway and falls into a hole. It's a deep, muddy hole and it takes him days to struggle out.

Some time later he's walking down the same pathway and reminds himself, 'Isn't there a hole here?', but just as he's thinking that he falls down the hole. It's a deep hole, but he's a little quicker out.

Some time later still, the traveller again comes to the same pathway and this time he's prepared. 'Don't fall down the hole,' he tells himself. 'It's right there.' But suddenly he hears a bird cawing from above. He glances up for a second and – bang – hits the bottom of the hole again. It doesn't seem so deep this time though and he's quickly out.

Again the traveller comes down the pathway and again he falls, but each time he does it, he's quicker to get out.

Until one day the traveller chooses to take a different pathway altogether.

This is a parable about awareness and what it takes for us to change our behaviours. So often with public speaking it feels like we're falling down a hole – with our nervous quirks, funny fidgets or shaky vocals. But with time and patience we can learn to drop the unhelpful habits and pick up those that inspire an audience.

What is perfect awareness?

- Getting in charge of 'the hole' of your nerves so that old mental patterns don't throw you off your power.
- Being conscious of what you're saying and how you're saying it, as you're saying it.
- Being in control of your body and speech, so that they don't detract from what you're saying.
- Choosing to use your full range of expression to enhance your public speaking message.

The stages of awareness

Awareness comes in four stages. You may be at different stages of awareness with different aspects of your speaking. Some behaviours may be conscious, whereas others might be hidden in a blind spot.

1. Blissfully unaware

Like our Edgar Mumble, most speakers who don't look for help are completely unaware of what they're doing wrong. They're satisfied with their performance, but from the audience's perspective they have embarrassing or distracting habits like fidgets and shuffles. To step beyond this stage takes the bravery to ask, 'How am I doing?'

2. Rude awakening

The answer to that question may not be a pleasant one. As you become more aware of your public speaking behaviours, you will notice habits you don't like. You'll see the gap between your abilities and the speaker you want to be. It can be difficult to hear, but the rude awakening is crucial to help you pro-

gress. If you don't have a single rude awakening during this book, then you probably haven't been honest with yourself.

3. Awkward ability

Then, as you become aware of what needs to change, you'll start to develop some new behaviours in your body language and vocal delivery. This phase is like learning to drive – you're changing the gears, but you have to think about it to get it right. You will see that you're improving, but you may also feel self-conscious.

4. Absorbed expertise

With time and practice, a new behaviour will become a natural part of your public speaking that you're no longer aware of. It feels great to perform like an expert without even realising it. Then it's time to pick the next bit of your performance to work on.

Anyone who continues to develop their awareness will become not just a competent speaker but a brilliant speaker. The difference between those who make it and those who stop halfway is their reaction during the rude awakening and awkward ability phases. At these stages your confidence can take a dip as you realise you have work to do to improve your public speaking. It's by pushing through these difficult moments that you'll learn how to inspire others.

In this part we'll investigate some rude awakenings in your public speaking habits and how awareness can bring choice regarding your nerves, body language and vocal delivery.

Chapter

Key wisdom from this chapter

- **Awareness brings choice:** when you become aware of your body language and vocal habits you can choose the behaviours that benefit your audience and drop the habits that are a bit weird.

- **You don't look as nervous as you feel:** the audience see perhaps 20% of the nerves that you're experiencing in your body.

- **Our public speaking beliefs become reality:** if we think positively of ourselves in public speaking we can reinforce our abilities, rather than giving extra energy to our weaknesses and doubt.

- **It's not about you:** even though it may feel like it. Public speaking is really about the audience in the room. If you seek to benefit them, rather than focusing on yourself, you will not only do a better job but your nerves will dissolve.

- **There's no such thing as 'perfect' public speaking:** we don't want you to memorise hundreds of facts, we'd rather you were a human being we can connect with.

The causes of fear

Some 70% of the population experience communication anxiety when asked to deliver a speech, according to researcher James McCroskey and his team.[2] If we can become aware of the root causes of fear, we can do something to stop ourselves from always slipping down the same hole.

What is public speaking fear?

Research into performance anxiety in music[3] has shown that there are four state changes that fear can cause. You may experience all or some of these in your public speaking:

1. Emotion: feeling nervous, stressed, worried or panicked.
2. Thought: forgetting your words or losing concentration.
3. Behaviour: trembling, fidgeting, moving in an awkward way.
4. Physiology: upset breathing, faster heartbeat or an upset stomach.

By understanding that these are symptoms of public speaking fear, you can get distance from them. Next time you're asked to speak in public and you find you have an upset stomach, you can realise that it's a natural and common experience.

It's also heartening to know that you're not alone. When we run our beginners' course and speakers get up to speak for the first time, they almost universally tell me: 'That was awful', 'I was shaking', 'I was blushing', 'I was waffling' and so on. The good news is that the audience see maybe 20% of whatever nerves you're feeling in the body. The difference in perception is simply that you're inside your body, feeling every wobble, whereas members of the audience are outside your body admiring you for daring to get up and speak.

> **Public speaking myth**
>
> *People fear public speaking more than death*
>
> Public speaking is often cited as people's biggest fear, with death featuring third or seventh, depending on the source. While this was reported in 1973 by one survey,[4] this information has never been verified by scholarly sources. It's not to say that public speaking isn't scary, but let's keep it in proportion.

When does fear happen?

Research into public speaking fear[5] found two different patterns of anxiety: physiological (body stuff, like heart rate increase, shaky limbs, shortness of breath, etc. – see Chapter 3) and psychological (mental stuff like worrying, doubting, over-preparing and so on).

Psychological anxiety peaks early in the days and weeks before your speech – perhaps when you're asked to speak, or when you start preparing and are worrying about what might go wrong.

Physiological anxiety tends to peak at the moment you step up on stage for the first time and begin to speak. Of course, the body stuff and the mental stuff are closely connected, but we'll examine how to become aware of – and in control of – both types of anxiety.

Psychological fear – five causes and remedies

Cause 1: Negative self-talk

We all have an inner dialogue going on almost constantly through our waking hours that tells us how we're doing in relation to the world around us. Psychologists call this 'self-talk'. Often, we aren't even aware of what we're telling ourselves, but it's still there, bubbling under the surface.

Research has shown[6] that positive self-talk improves success in sports as varied as tennis, darts and figure skating, and that negative self-talk reduces the chances of success. The same seems to be the case for public speaking.

Imagine the public speaker who steps on stage having spent the past two days thinking, 'I'm boring, I'll forget what I'm going to say, they won't like me.' How will his confidence be affected? His self-talk will affect his posture and the way he talks, so that the feedback he gets from his audience will reinforce his belief. 'That's why I'm afraid of public speaking' will be his triumphant declaration over a glass of whisky later that evening. 'I told you I was no good at it.'

This comes from the part of our brain known as the reticular activating system, which shows us more of whatever we focus on. Let's say you buy a new red coat, thinking nobody else you know owns one. You put on the coat with glee as you leave the shop. And as you step outside, what's the first thing you see? Red coats all over the place.

What you place your attention on, your brain spots more of. The same goes for public speaking. Focus on the negatives and your brain will point out all the reasons you're terrible at speaking and present it as a fact.

The good news is that the same works in reverse, so if you can counteract the self-talk you can help to build your confidence.

Remedy for negative self-talk

Step 1: Get aware of the self-talk. If you can't spot it, you can't change it. My self-talk was always about not being good enough, specifically that I was too young for this when I started. I used to spend hours over-preparing to combat the inadequacy I felt and always felt someone would spot that I shouldn't be there. This is called 'impostor syndrome' and I've encountered it in all walks of life, among all sorts of people from recent graduates to CEOs.

Step 2: The 'so what' approach. We avoid public speaking because we're terrified of the self-talk being proved right. Yet if we can diminish the thing we're afraid of, it can't hurt us any more. Try these for size:

'I'm too young'	→	'So what if I am?'
'I do not know enough'	→	'So what if I don't?'
'I might blush'	→	'So what if I do?'
'I might be boring'	→	'So what if I am?'

This approach gives you permission to take your negative self-talk less seriously and to reduce its hold on you.

Step 3: Reframing and owning. Change the emphasis of your self-talk into a positive phrase that will help your speaking. Within every fear there is a positive perspective:

'I'm too young'	→	'I'm playful, let's use that!'
'I do not know enough'	→	'I don't need to know everything'
'I might blush'	→	'Blushing is a sign I'm passionate'
'I might be boring'	→	'Whatever happens, I really care about this message'

Find a positive reframe for your negative self-talk and then practise using it every time you slip down your hole.

Cause 2: The egocentric speaker

When you're standing on stage it's easy to think it's all about you. Everyone's looking at you, so they must be listening to every word you say and critiquing every moment. This is the

habit of the egocentric speaker. From this perspective it's easy to feel attacked by the audience.

Research shows[7] a connection between the level of fear experienced and the amount a speaker focuses on themselves. This means that the more a speaker worries about their lines, their performance and their visual aids, the more anxious they will feel.

Of course, there is a mistake here, which is easily resolved. Think about last time you were in an audience. Who did you care more about, yourself or the speaker? Honestly, it was yourself, right? That's not to say you're uniquely selfish, rather that most people in the audience are so wrapped up in their own stuff that what the speaker is doing is secondary. Sure, audience members want a confident, knowledgeable speaker, but they want it for their own sake so they can benefit. They see maybe 20% of whatever nerves you're feeling and they certainly don't know what you've planned to say.

So, get over yourself! Although it may seem like it, public speaking really isn't about you: it's about your audience.

Remedy for egocentric speaking

Get over your egocentric terror by developing the mindset of a servant speaker. We'll come back to this in Chapter 5.

The servant speaker forgets about herself and realises that the people listening also have needs. When you stop worrying about yourself, your nerves slide away and you do a better job of meeting the audience's needs.

Cause 3: Perfectionism

A third source/cause of fear can be your personality type. I sometimes see nervous public speakers over-preparing for speeches, or avoiding speaking full stop 'until I'm ready'. Cognitive behavioural science has shown a connection between perfectionism and fear. Perfectionists who look to their audience to determine how well they did experience more anxiety.

If you have any of the following habits then you could be a perfectionist:

- Taking failure to heart.
- Ruminating over failure, even a long time after it has passed.
- Turning one failure, 'I failed on this occasion', into a generalisation, 'I am a failure'.
- Treating ambiguous or neutral feedback as negative.

Perfectionists rely heavily on their success to feel a sense of self-worth, so if they fail or are worried that they will fail, they will experience a high degree of distress or anxiety. Although we sneakily think that it's good to be a perfectionist, research shows otherwise.[8] In a variety of situations the perfectionist performs less well than the person who gives it a shot.

Remedy for perfectionism

You can't learn to speak French without ordering a few croissants. Get out and speak *before* you feel ready to test your material. You'll learn what works and what to improve on. The extra practice you get will make you a much better speaker than if you try to get everything right first time.

Cause 4: Catastrophising

Catastrophising is over-emphasising the possible negative outcomes of public speaking. If you believe you're likely to fail, you are more likely to experience public speaking anxiety. Research shows[9] that it's what we understand to be the consequences of failure that makes us feel most nervous. We grossly exaggerate what's at stake with our public speaking.

Catastrophising thoughts are often hidden somewhere, just below the rational surface of our mind. Even if we know our fears to be logically impossible, deep down we believe the risks to be genuine possibilities. Do any of these thoughts sound familiar?

If I mess up, I'll . . .

look like an idiot

ruin the whole event

get the sack

cause a major embarrassment to so-and-so

lose out on an opportunity permanently.

Psychologists have classified these thoughts into five distinct fears of failure:

1. Fear of experiencing shame and embarrassment.
2. Fear of not meeting your own standards.
3. Fear of having an uncertain future as a result of your performance.
4. Fear of important others losing interest in you/what you're saying.
5. Fear of upsetting important others.

The more we focus on these possibilities, the bigger they become in our mind. Soon we see no other option than a dramatic failure and we'll do anything to get out of facing an audience.

People around you will also contribute to intensifying the risk of a public speaking situation, perhaps due to their own vicarious fear. When you combine your own fear of failure with the fear of failure that others harbour, the risks seem both very serious indeed and very likely to happen.

Remedy for catastrophising

If the risk is high we often become exceptionally tense, switching off the creative and flexible parts of our brain. In this way we actually make the 'catastrophe' more likely to happen. To counteract this tendency:

1. Become aware of your catastrophising tendency. Are you secretly telling yourself that you *just might die* if you do this presentation?
2. Gently laugh at yourself. This is the best way to restore your creative functioning.

Cause 5: Seeing yourself small

Finally, your self-image also plays a role in building public speaking fear. Self-image is the mental picture you hold of yourself as a public speaker. Do you imagine yourself on stage as someone shining with confidence, or someone small and awkward-looking?

Speakers with high levels of anxiety are more likely to have a self-image that's negative and vague, in comparison with more confident speakers. They picture themselves as generally not that good at public speaking, but don't see the exact things that they're doing wrong (that's why awareness is so important).

Remedy for seeing yourself small

The crucial thing to remember is that your self-image isn't the same as how you actually come across to an audience. In my beginners' workshops I often watch speakers give a perfectly confident talk and then collapse back into their seats, complaining of how nervous they were and how terrible their performance was. Typically, the audience see you as doing much better than you think.

Where you view your self-image from is also important. Research shows[10] that nervous public speakers are more likely to recall themselves speaking from outside their body looking in, rather than from inside their body looking out. Notice your mental image and change it to a more empowered one.

Chapter

3

Key wisdom from this chapter

- **The predator reflex:** public speaking feels so scary because it evokes a situation where predators are watching you, the prey. This is a normal response that we can overcome.

- **Spot your anxiety habits:** fear can show up in your movements, gestures, posture, eye contact or vocal delivery. If you spot it, you can do something about it.

- **The five gateways to body confidence:** by finding the right posture, breathing, vision, facial expressions and reacting effectively to silence, we can teach our bodies that we are safe rather than under threat.

Finding safety in the body

The predator reflex

Standing in front of an audience evokes a physiological response similar to that of being under attack. Our body signals to us: 'All those eyes looking at you are predators . . . and they look hungry.' As a result the body's fight or flight mechanism is triggered. Our body's core processes, such as thinking, speaking and digesting, become deprioritised and adrenaline causes our limbs to tense, to get us ready to run away or fight. That's why we can experience stomach troubles in the lead-up to a big talk and that's why it can be difficult to think clearly, let alone speak sensibly, when we're put on the spot.

As this predator reflex goes on within the body, we're just standing on stage, trying to do a bit of public speaking. If we're not aware, the excess adrenaline can trigger a chain reaction that stops our body functioning naturally. Awkward habits show up that disconnect us from the audience. An untamed fidget can pull the attention of the audience away from what you're saying and give the perception that you're not confident. This will make the audience close off to your message and start to doubt you.

Five habits of physiological anxiety

This section outlines some of the key public speaking quirks to become aware of. Once you spot them you can do something about them.

1. Eye contact

Consider how easy it is to ignore or drift off from a video, a podcast or a conference call. Even when you're watching a live webcast of a speech or presentation, it's easier to drift off than if you were in the room. At least part of this is because of the lack of eye contact between you and the speaker.

When a speaker makes good eye contact with their audience, the audience feel like an exchange, a conversation, is taking place. In a conversation we expect to participate, so we listen more effectively.

Become aware of where your eyes are going as you speak:

- Do you see more of your audience's faces, or more of the ceiling, floor or window when you speak?
- Do you hang on to one friendly, supportive or important person in the room and forget to make eye contact with other parts of the audience?
- Are your eyes pulled down by your notes, or away to a PowerPoint presentation?

These are three ways in which you may disconnect from your audience. The impact can be bad – if the audience don't feel spoken to they will drift off into their own thoughts.

2. Fiddles and fidgets

With all that adrenaline in the body, the limbs can feel very awkward. Speakers are often uncertain what to do with their hands and if you're not careful, all sorts of distracting tendencies can come up.

To get aware, record yourself speaking, or get feedback. Check which of these quirks show up:

- **Scratchy, fiddly fidgets:** notice what your hands and feet do to cope with that extra adrenaline. Do you find yourself playing with your clothing, clicking a pen, scratching yourself or obsessively folding a piece of paper? If you're not aware of these habits, you can't do anything to stop them and they have the power to destroy a talk as the audience stop paying attention.

- **No hands:** some speakers combat the fidgets by hiding their hands – it could be by putting them behind their back or in a pocket. While less distracting than repetitive fidgets, you're creating a barrier to your audience and losing the possibility for expression.

- **Over-repetitive gestures:** sometimes we find a gesture that works well and then keep the body on 'repeat' mode indefinitely as we lose awareness. Any gesture that is used too much has the possibility to distract attention away from your message.

3. Movement

Adrenaline doesn't only affect our hands, it can also play havoc with our legs:

- **Jelly legs:** the very first time I spoke in public, my legs were quivering. I remember thinking, 'How can I speak when I can't even stand?' The good news is that this feeling passes quickly if you let it. Even better news is that your audience won't be able to see a quiver here and there, so you can put it out of your mind.

- **Need-the-loo feet:** nervous speakers often cross their legs or point their knees together slightly as a defence mechanism. To the audience it can look as though they are desperate for the loo – not exactly an empowered stance.

- **The rocking horse:** I once watched a managing director on stage, speaking to 200 of his clients, rocking back and forth from one foot to the other for 20 minutes. I couldn't concentrate on his words and I felt seasick by the end!

- **Dance floor grooves:** another time I watched a TEDx speaker do the same 'dance move' of three steps again and again for his whole talk. It's telling that this is all I could remember about his talk afterwards.

4. Posture

Another common physiological reaction to the threat of predators is to try to hide. Our body subconsciously strives to make
itself smaller, so that it's less of a target. This can show up in our
body in a variety of ways:

- **Shrinking from our full height:**
  there is a huge difference between
  a speaker who stands proudly at
  their full height and one whose
  posture is pinched and contracted.
  The former gives confidence to
  themselves and to their audience
  and the latter quickly loses credibility. (More on this in the next
  section.)

- **Hiding on the stage:** another
  method of ducking the predators
  is to position yourself to the side
  of the stage, behind a lectern, just
  behind a flipchart stand, or to focus
  your attention on the PowerPoint
  presentation behind you. These are
  strategies for shifting the attention
  of the audience away from you. The chances are the audience
  will notice you less, but that's no good thing. If you're trying to
  persuade or inspire an audience, your personal impact is key.

- **Defensive barriers:** finally, if there's no place to hide, you
  might find yourself protecting yourself behind a crossed leg,
  folded arms, or even your notes. Any of these methods blocks
  you from your audience and can make the nerves worse still.

As you shrink the body, you may squash your lungs, making it more
difficult to breathe naturally. Oxygen has a passifying effect on the
fight or flight mechanism, so we need every deep breath we can take.

5. Vocal spluttering

The fight or flight response also affects your voice. Your
breathing becomes more shallow and your voice isn't needed –
after all, you're running away from a predator, not having a
conversation with it. This can lead to:

- **rushed speaking:** as we hurry to get away from such a traumatic setting
- **fillers:** such as constant 'ums' and 'erms', which are designed as a protective tool to stop our audience from jumping in. This is, of course, a hangover from one-to-one communication as no audience member would really cut you off mid-sentence
- **dull expression:** the more expressive you are, the more you will be noticed and the more of a target you are for the public speaking predator. That's why you often see speakers removing all personality and expression when they speak
- **timid volume:** another way to hide is for your audience not to hear you. Be aware if you have a soft voice, or if people are craning to hear you at the back.

Safety in the body

If nervous habits show up, it's because we don't feel safe on a physiological level, says non-verbal communication expert Luke Gregorczyk.[11] These nervous habits in turn make the audience feel less certain about our speaking abilities, which can create a negative spiral that makes us feel even less confident.

Gregorczyk advises the following embodied approach to creating confidence.

Start by noticing your quirks

As we were doing above, get aware of any strange quirks and habits in your body. These are clues that your body doesn't feel safe. At all moments we are subconsciously scanning our environment for potential threats. This happens at the oldest levels of our nervous system (the limbic system and the reptilian brain) and can be influenced only through the body.

Gregorczyk says there are five main 'gateways' of the body that can help us to step into safety. Through accessing these gateways the body brings us a sense of reassurance that signals 'I am safe' and allows us the feeling of being 'at home' on stage. This is when we're the most creative and inspiring as speakers.

The five gateways to body confidence

Gateway 1: posture

The part of our nervous system that determines our safety is located in front of our spine. It needs support to feel safe. If the spine is poorly supported by the legs and/or the pelvis, you'll get feedback from your nervous system that you're not safe. That's why it's often suggested that we place our feet 'firmly planted on ground and shoulder width apart'. When you feel fully grounded it's because your feet really are connecting firmly with the ground – simple!

The most vulnerable part of your body is the stomach area, as it's not protected by the skeleton. Some speakers try to hide that area behind a lectern or set of notes, making them seem defensive. To make yourself feel safe rather than defensive, Gregorczyk suggests giving yourself a 'gentle hug' to the belly just before you start speaking and releasing it as you feel safe.

Gateway 2: breath

Probably the most important aspect of bodily safety, the breath tells us whether we're in danger or not. Shallow breathing activates the fight or flight response, whereas deep breathing stimulates the parasympathetic nervous system, which is responsible for the feeling of safety in the body. When you feel under pressure, consciously allow your breath to go deeper in your body. Release your breath slowly on the exhale and you'll start to feel safer. Five minutes of focused breathing in the loo before you speak can make the world of difference to your confidence. Then connect it to your posture and you're on to a winner.

Top tip

This is an excellent way to counteract negative thoughts, as we described in Chapter 2. When those thoughts show up, simply return to your breath and let them pass. This of course takes practice, so don't be discouraged.

Gateway 3: vision

Fight or flight naturally disposes us towards tunnel vision as we're looking for a way out of a dangerous situation. In speaking, this might mean focusing on one 'negative' person in the audience, or staring at a point of 'escape' out of the window. It disconnects us from our audience and places our attention on the things we fear – creating a vicious circle.

Break this habit by noticing what is at the left and right of the room. Embrace the whole of the room, as if a floodlight has been switched on. You'll find this helps you to disengage from fight or flight because you start to see your fear as just one element in the bigger picture of your environment.

Gateway 4: hearing – our reaction to silence

When danger is present, humans and animals are wired to fall silent. It happens when a waiter drops a plate in a restaurant – everyone instinctively falls silent for a moment to check whether danger is present. The same response is triggered when the audience falls silent – our body tells us we are under threat.

To break this, try one of two methods:

1. **Hearing a human voice:** there's a link between the human voice and the feeling of safety. Starting your speech with an interactive question will stop the warning lights flashing.

2. **Break the ice of silence with laughter:** whether it's a joke or something you do to make yourself chuckle, laughter signals to your body that the threat has passed. You'll notice the same happening after the plate has been dropped in a restaurant – a moment of startled silence, followed by cheers or laughter.

Gateway 5: facial expression

We often hear that the face is the mirror of the soul and evolutionarily speaking, this seems to be the case. In fact, it has been proved that facial communication is older than language. When our audience smile and laugh, we feel accepted as part of the community. But when we don't receive feedback from them, our safety mechanism fires a danger signal/alarm.

The question then is: how can we encourage our audience to feel safe or relaxed enough to express positive emotions through their facial expressions? It's difficult for one human being to be unmoved when another smiles at them. If you lead by having open and positive facial expressions towards your audience, they will be more likely to respond with signals of acceptance. And even if they don't, smiling signals to your system that you're safe and the nerves will begin to relax.

Of course, each of these gateways to body confidence take awareness to access. Remember that even if you continually fall down the same hole, the way out is correct. Over time you will get out faster and faster – and one day you'll even avoid the hole completely.

Chapter

Key wisdom from this chapter

- **When the body feels safe, it is more creative:** so only when we've handled the fight or flight response can we look to being more inspiring speakers.

- **Credibility comes from the body:** look for solid posture, definite movement, a slow, assertive pace and powerful pausing if you want more gravitas in your speaking.

- **Charisma comes from the body:** if you want to energise your audience, use dynamic gestures, movement, vocal range and passion in your body language and voice.

- **Connect with your audience:** use inclusive gestures, connective eye contact and pauses if you'd like to involve your audience more in your talk.

Expression in the body and voice

Once you've found safety in the body, your nervous system functioning switches to the newer, creative part of the brain known as the neo-cortex. Only now will you have the capacity to fully choose how you express yourself and what type of impact you bring to your audience. Exactly what type of expression you choose will depend on:

- **the speaking situation:** your expression will differ vastly between a eulogy and a motivational speech
- **your intention:** do you wish to lift the energy of the audience, or ground it in something serious?
- **your style:** different types of expression suit different people. Your style should always feel authentic to you rather than a mimic of someone else's technique.

As we'll see in Part 5, public speaking is an act of leadership. By varying your expression you can have whatever impact you choose. Here are some ideas for how you might use your body language and vocal delivery to have your intended impact. Remember that these are not rules of public speaking but ideas for you to play with and apply in a way that suits your personality.

Impact 1: bringing credibility

Perhaps you're keen to get the audience to trust you and your message. Credibility is important at the beginning of a talk and also when you are hitting home your key message. This is the territory of speakers with gravitas, such as Nelson Mandela or Winston Churchill. It is especially useful in business presentations or on solemn occasions. To give yourself more credibility as a speaker, look to emphasise the following tendencies in your body:

GRAVITAS & CREDIBILITY

1. **A solid body:** as explained above, safety in the body will elicit trust from the audience. At your key moments of influence, stand rock solid and still in your body, rooted to the ground. Think *bulldog*.

2. **Intentional gestures:** look for powerful movements that are solid and intentional. You might try:
   - palm-down gestures to create certainty and close an argument
   - precise slicing gestures to divide the components of an argument
   - deliberate gestures which then return to a neutral spot for your hands
   - occasional assertive gestures such as a fist in the hand.

3. **Solid eye contact:** eye contact creates trust. To assert your credibility, hold eye contact a little longer than usual to ensure that your audience feel your belief in your topic.

4. **Pacing:** a slow, assertive speed of speaking will help the audience grasp the importance of your message. Resist the urge to rush through your talk and let the audience hear. Every. Word.

5. **Powerful pauses:** at key moments in your talk use silence to emphasise your message. When you're building credibility, what you *don't* say is as important as what you do say. I call this a 'powerful pause' and it feels a little like a bungee jump: scary but exhilarating. Try this:

- Find your most important point.
- Deliver it with power.
- And . . . shut up.
- Wait.
- Wait a little more.
- Feel the audience react.
- Then talk.

Silence can turn a mundane talk into one that's inspiring.

Impact 2: creating energy

If you want to inspire people to buy into an idea or project you will need to enthuse them. This is the territory of passionate, dynamic and charismatic speaking. Think of charismatic speakers like Martin Luther King Jr or John F. Kennedy. These are some of the characteristics that help to uplift the audience:

ENERGY & CHARISMA

1. **Dynamic gestures:** speakers often use a very limited space with their gestures. To create movement and energy:

   - use your full horizontal range to demonstrate the size or scope of an issue
   - remember that the more you raise your hands, the more energy you produce. Typically, gestures above your head evoke the body language of a preacher or motivational speaker
   - vary your gestures to match your specific point. Bring moments of small, precise gestures to match a detail and moments of large and energetic gestures to evoke passion
   - be sure to keep your gestures intentional and solid – too much flappy movement adds confusion rather than energy.

2. **Movement:**

   - Where stillness brings credibility, too much stillness can lose energy. Keep your audience engaged by moving with intention across the stage.
   - You might design different parts of the stage for different messages. For example, the audience's left (your right) might be something that's in the past or something bad, and the audience's right (your left) might be something in the future or something good.
   - Don't be constrained by the stage – some of the best motivational speakers, like Tony Robbins, move into the audience to keep up the energy.

3. **Vocal range:** if you've ever sat through listening to a speaker with a monotone, robotic voice, you'll know it's one of the worst traumas for an audience. Monotone expression is easy to get into when we're explaining something complicated, or the topic is dull. In contrast, varied intonation can bring dry topics alive and bring drama to stories and anecdotes. To increase your vocal range, try practising your speech to a child as if you're telling them a story. If you can keep their interest through great vocal range, you're onto a winner.

4. **Pacing:** in contrast to the slow and deliberate pacing of credible expression, moments of speed add energy to a talk. A faster pace is useful when you're trying to

encourage, or at moments of excitement in a story. Be careful not to go too far though – we still need to understand and absorb your words.

5. **Passion and belief:** the audience can hear if you believe in your message, yet often we're scared of showing our passion in case other people sneer. Ask yourself this: how many times have you left a talk feeling deflated and complaining, 'Urgh, that speaker was dull'? Often, I'd guess. And how many times have you left a talk complaining, 'Urgh, that speaker was too passionate'? Probably never. Our audience crave much more energy and passion than we imagine.

Impact 3: creating connection

You might also wish to bring your audience into your talk and make them feel part of a conversation. Speakers in this mode of expression are described as empathetic, connective or warm.

CONNECTION

1. **Inclusive gestures:** to connect your audience to your message, try some of these gestures:
   - Use open-palmed gestures to encourage participation or thought.
   - Suggest participating by signalling to a member of the audience that you'd like their thoughts. Usually pointing

with your whole hand is less aggressive than directly with one finger.

- Alter the level of energy in the room by lifting or lowering your gestures. Lifting brings the energy to interact, whereas lowering signals a more reflective engagement.

2. **Connective eye contact:** connection is key in this mode, so look for sparkly, connective eye contact that creates a bond with individual audience members. Suggest with your eye contact, 'I'm interested in you, you're part of this', even if you're speaking to a large audience who can't respond.

3. **Pause for thought:** a speaker who seeks to engage discussion will often ask questions to the audience. This doesn't work unless you leave enough space for your audience to respond. Pausing creates a more reflective atmosphere.

Truly inspiring speakers are able to use all three types of expression as they choose. Of course, there are other types of expression beyond these three and I encourage you to experiment with what combination of body language and vocal variety best serves your audience.

Part

2

It's not how strongly you feel about your topic,
it's how strongly they feel about your topic
after you speak.

Tim Salladay

Edgar Mumble looked at the feedback forms from his audience and scratched his head. Then he frowned. 'Pah! How dare they say my talk was boring?' he scoffed. 'What do these people know anyway? I've studied this subject for 15 years. They were begging me to do the talk. They clearly haven't got a clue.'

Edgar looked around the office to see if anyone was looking and slid the feedback sheets into the bin.

Empathy

In Part 2:

- How to completely switch your mindset away from self-obsession and towards serving your audience.

- The power of preparing with your audience in mind and how to do it successfully.

- How to give your audience what they need (rather than only what they want).

- Tips for managing difficult audience members.

- How to frame a talk so that everyone wants to listen.

A basic equation, if you will. Next time you're engaged in a piece of public speaking, count the number of people on stage speaking at any one time. Then count the number of people in the audience.

Which is the greater number? Assuming you're not having a real public speaking nightmare, I'd imagine the audience number is greater, right? So who does it make more sense to focus on, yourself, the speaker, or the x number of people in the audience?

SPEAKER = 1   **AUDIENCE MEMBERS = 1 + ...**

Empathy means prioritising your audience and putting them at the heart of your talk. It is something that speakers forget consistently. Why? Because we so easily get stuck in the egocentric speaker tendency I mentioned in Chapter 2. We're being looked at, so we imagine we're being scrutinised. We start worrying about our content (what do I want to say?), our personality (am I good enough?), even our clothing (do I look professional enough?). And we completely forget about our audience.

Speakers who drop their ego and step into the mindset of the servant speaker will engage the audience and connect them deeply to the topic. They answer the audience's concerns and questions just as if they were mind readers. They have the audience buzzing with a feeling of 'Yes! That's me!' combined with the resonance of 'Wow! This is really helpful!'.

The egocentric speaker

- Constantly thinks of the speech in terms of 'me' or 'I'. Even when you think you're over it and ask yourself to focus on the audience, you still have to take care. The egocentric speaker may think, 'Yes, let's focus on the audience . . . I wonder what they think about ME.' This is still egocentric!
- Can be more nervous or self-obsessive because they see themselves as under attack from the audience.
- Misses clues about how the audience are feeling.
- Ends up being *less* impressive because the audience's needs aren't considered.

The servant speaker

- Knows and understands the needs of their audience.
- Understands how the audience feels about the topic – and meets them there.
- Manages hopes, needs and expectations so that different types of audience members are satisfied.
- Lets personal judgement of the audience slide and instead thinks, 'How can I help these people?'

With no empathy, a speaker ends up with an audience who are against them. Like Edgar Mumble's audience, this could mean silence and negative feedback. Or a lack of empathy could lead to awkward questions, rude comments and even people walking out of the room.

How do you know you have empathy?

As you start to develop empathy with your audience you'll notice positive effects, such as:

- audience members listening more intently and contributing in ways that seem to further your aims
- indications that the audience relate to your message, such as:
  - shining eyes
  - nodding
  - strong eye contact

- laughter with your humour
- enthusiastic participation.

• comments in feedback forms like 'that was spot on', 'just what I wanted' and 'it answered all my questions'
• your own speaking experience feeling easier or more pleasant.

Research gives two reasons why empathy is so important. Social psychologists describe the feeling of closeness between an information giver (the speaker) and receiver (the audience) as 'immediacy'.[12] If an audience feels more immediacy towards the speaker, they will learn more effectively. Second, as developments in neuroscience are showing, there is a positive link between the emotional state of your audience and the amount they learn.[13] In other words, happy audience members literally store and retain more information.

Powerful empathy and breaking rapport

However, a word of caution is needed. It's possible to be so 'matey' or informal that you are empathising with your audience at the expense of your material, for instance understanding their difficulties so much that you don't tell them the true and powerful solution.

There's a Tibetan parable about a little boy who is stuck down a well. His mother hears his cries and finds him cold and alone all the way down at the bottom. And she is so saddened by her lonely little boy that she jumps down the well to be with him.

Of course, the mother should run and get a rope to pull the boy out of the well. It's obvious. Yet sometimes we 'jump down the well' to be with our audience as we want to be liked by them. Your purpose as an inspiring speaker is not to be liked, it is to create change. Sometimes change can feel difficult, or unpopular. True empathy is to wish to benefit your audience when you speak and to do whatever is necessary to get there. We'll return to this idea in Part 5.

How do you develop empathy?

Developing empathy is a process of looking at public speaking in a different way. The shift from egocentric to servant speaking may be natural for you, or it may take some practice. Once you've learned this shift in mindset, it will remain strong. You will begin to know instinctively how to build empathy with an audience and your public speaking will benefit dramatically as a result.

This part focuses on the following tools to build empathy:

1. Before you speak:
   - empathetic preparation
   - setting up your environment.
2. During and after your talk:
   - setting agreements with your audience
   - different audience types and what to do with them
   - breaking rapport for impact
   - holding empathy beyond your performance.

Chapter

5

Key wisdom from this chapter

- **Public speaking is about the audience, not you:** although it may seem as though everyone's judging you, the audience is most interested in how *they* will benefit from your talk. Focus on this and you'll be more confident and more effective as a speaker.

- **Prepare by getting into the audience's heads:** the best speakers think from the perspective of the audience and design their talk from there.

- **The audience want to be in your talk:** spot the ways they want to be recognised and include these in your talk.

- **Set up your room to meet the audience's needs:** it's your responsibility to make sure the room is set up to give the audience the best chance of understanding and remembering what you have to say.

Preparing with empathy

The mindset of the servant speaker

Egocentric speaking is such a strong tendency that it requires awareness and practice to counteract.

Empathy versus rapport

Consider that the choice of the word 'empathy' rather than 'rapport' is deliberate.

- Empathy is defined as *understanding and entering into another's feelings.*
- Rapport is defined as *a relationship of mutual understanding or trust and agreement between people.*

Rapport is a give-and-take relationship, whereas empathy is giving understanding without expecting to receive any in return. We're all good at the 'me' part of rapport, but we typically neglect the 'they' of the audience.

Imagine the pre-performance thought process of a speaker focused on rapport:

Will they like me? Will I be able to get eye contact with them? Will they understand my argument? Will they laugh at my jokes?

This speaker's got it part right, because she's at least thinking about her audience. But she is relating everything back to herself, which makes her nervous and over-analytical about what she should or shouldn't put in her speech. Change the focus to empathy and her thought process will be more like this:

What can I give my audience to help them enjoy this? What do they need? How could this be structured to help them understand? What kind of humour would go down well?

The empathetic speaker doesn't 'manipulate' her audience to suit her aims, but honestly and authentically aims to serve. With empathy, you create so much connection to the audience that they receive your message in a more positive way. And as you focus on building empathy towards your audience, you worry less and less about yourself.

Empathetic preparation

To get into the mindset of your audience takes the right sort of preparation. Often we prepare by listing all the key points we want to get across, when much of that can be irrelevant or boring to the audience. If we instead shift the emphasis to serving the audience, the content that comes out will be closer to meeting their needs.

How much preparation do I need to do?

When you speak about a new topic, or are speaking to a new audience, you will probably need to do lots of preparation to develop the most engaging and enjoyable talk you can – more on this in Parts 3 and 4. The key is to use your preparation time in a smart way to connect to the most relevant content for your audience, otherwise you can waste a lot of time.

You can get into the empathetic mindset by asking yourself questions about:

1. **The audience's perception of your topic:** what are the expectations or preconceived ideas the audience hold about your subject matter?
2. **The audience on you:** what do the audience want or need from you as a speaker?
3. **The audience on the audience:** the needs the audience hold towards themselves as individuals and as a group.

1. The audience on the topic

As soon as a speech, presentation or workshop is given a title, the audience will hold a host of assumptions about how the talk will be. For example, if you watch TED Talks (see www.ted.com if you haven't), you'll notice that you have a reaction depending on the subject itself.

Have a look at some TED Talk titles and you'll get an idea of your gut reaction to different topics:

- 'What our hallucinations reveal about our minds.'
- 'On DNA and the sea.'
- 'Investing in Africa's own solutions.'
- 'A feminine response to Iceland's financial crash.'
- 'We can avoid aging.'
- 'A leap from the edge of space.'
- 'How to expose the corrupt.'
- 'Why not eat insects?'

Notice how some of these topics will interest you more than others? Some of them will sound fun, technical or intriguing and some you may know something about already. Some titles may sound boring to you. Your audience go through exactly the same process in judging your topic or title.

Consider what your audience might know about your topic

Do your audience perceive the topic as exciting or boring? How many people will see this topic as important to them and how many are less concerned about it? How many people consider themselves beginners and how many think they're experts? Although you may not know for sure until you're in the room, these questions are designed to help you plan in the way that best empathises with the audience you anticipate.

You can find out more about your audience by:

- asking presenters who have faced a similar audience
- asking members of your audience (if you are able to) what their expectations and assumptions are about the topic
- finding out the 'popular opinion' about your subject from blog articles, newspapers, etc.
- asking the audience during your talk (risky if you do this alone)
- trial and error.

Look at the diagram below and ask yourself where your audience sit on each scale.

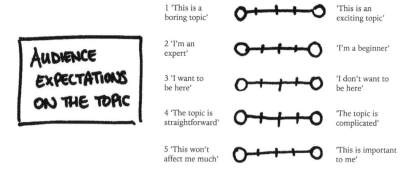

Once you've judged your audience's place on each scale, you will have a map of their expectations on the topic. The more you prepare, the better equipped you'll be to handle every situation you may face, even if there are some tricky characters in the audience (more on this in the next chapter).

Here's how you might use the information to prepare or tailor your information.

1. Boring topic vs exciting topic

If you're presenting a topic that people usually consider boring, such as health and safety, or finances, what can you do to change their minds? Bring more dynamic expression (Chapter 4) and develop freshness (Chapter 9) to jazz up your delivery. You could connect a health and safety talk to stories of people's lives being saved and you could see financial figures as stories of how the company's doing, for example.

If people are likely to be excited by your topic, you have both a bonus and a possible danger. The bonus is that there will be a positive energy in the room and your audience will take less effort to energise. The danger is that if their expectations are not met and you deliver in a way that's less exciting than expected, you may disappoint.

Always aim to excite your audience in a way that's authentic to you. Excitement could mean bouncing around the stage enthusiastically, just as it could mean giving intelligent insight on a topic or invoking strong emotions through storytelling.

2. Experts vs beginners

It's crucial to know the knowledge level of your audience when you're delivering any kind of information-focused speech or presentation. If you pitch your content too low, your audience will leave feeling they've learned nothing. If you pitch too high, they'll be lost. Get it right and it will feel like you're exactly meeting their needs.

Sometimes it's easy to see the knowledge level of an audience, but if there are people at different knowledge levels you will need to stay flexible during your talk to determine which level is the best for the group as a whole. Sometimes you'll have the opportunity to survey your audience on their knowledge levels and expectations for a talk, in which case treat that information as gold dust.

But if you have no way of researching your audience's expertise, then use your best guess to create a Plan A. Also prepare Plan B material that you can use if your audience have more, or less, knowledge than you thought. Before you launch into presenting your content, ask your audience some questions to judge their level. Try, 'How many of you have heard something about neurology before?' if you want a hands-up answer, or 'What do you know about neurology?' if you want more detailed information. If your Plan A is wrong, it's then easy to adjust.

3. 'I want to be here' vs 'I'm only here because I have to be'

It's important to understand the likely motivation of your audience. Are your audience schoolchildren, employees or another group who have been forced to listen to you speak, or are they listening to you of their own accord? This will affect the degree to which you need to 'sell' the concept of your talk to them.

If you have an audience who have low motivation towards your topic, make sure you get them involved in the topic as soon as possible. Find a way that works for you. I use fun and interaction a lot, especially when I work with young people (competitions and sweets work particularly well in this situation). Other speakers use colourful storytelling to show that this topic is relevant to the audience, while others use their own brand of humour to get people interested. The important thing for low-motivation groups is to make them feel part of your talk. Show them how they fit into the topic. Use their language.

For audiences who have chosen to hear you speak, reward and praise their enthusiasm. High-motivation groups can usually be relied upon to ask questions and interact with you. Use their enthusiasm to go deeper into the material than you usually would – they will lap up any information you have to give them.

4. 'The topic is straightforward' vs 'The topic is complicated'

If many people in an audience perceive the topic as complicated, there may be an air of tension or confusion in the room, even before you start speaking. Mention accountancy, particle physics or property law to your average Joe and you'll see a reaction that indicates their discomfort with the subject.

It's important to get underneath this discomfort to see precisely what it relates to. Are they uncomfortable because they expect technical concepts that they don't understand? Are they uncomfortable because of the type of people involved with the profession? Where are they getting their information and stereotypes on your topic from?

This information will help you knock aside barriers to listening before they've even arisen in the minds of the audience. This is how some speakers seem to mind-read. They use the language of their audience to turn the complexity of the subject into something they can relate to.

One accountant I know works with small, creative businesses. She starts her presentations with:

We like you to think accountancy's difficult, but the secret is it's really a piece of cake. If we told you that, we wouldn't have a job!

This instantly puts a tense audience at ease and allows them to soak up more information than if they were expecting not to understand the speaker.

You may have people at the other end of this spectrum, who think the topic is a piece of cake. In this case think about how you want to use that information. Perhaps you'd like to challenge them to see your topic isn't as set in stone as they think. Perhaps you'd like those who find it straightforward to help or work with others who struggle with the topic. Perhaps you'd prefer to split the audience into one group who find your topic simple and another with people who want to go at a slower pace. Think creatively about how best to serve their needs.

5. 'This won't affect me much' vs 'This is important to me'

An audience who think what you're saying is important to them will listen harder and for longer. So ask yourself what it is that your audience as a group really care about and then relate your topic to these things.

There was a fantastic example of this when finance guru Alvin Hall was brought in to teach maths to a group of disaffected teens. Rather than launch in with mathematical theory, he told them his rags-to-riches story from a childhood of crushing poverty to his current fame and fortune. When he linked this back to a basic understanding of maths, you can bet he suddenly had their full attention.

So the steps for demonstrating importance of your topic are:

1. Using stories and examples to which your audience can relate.
2. Providing compelling reasons for them to find what you have to say important.
3. Using their language (whether they're teenagers or business managers) to get the message across.

Also, if you treat your topic as important, your energy will encourage the audience to feel the same way about it.

The audience on your topic

Putting the picture together

Now you've established your audience's expectations of your topic, think how that affects your performance:

- How much time should I take?
- How much content is needed?
- What are the best examples, anecdotes and 'fizzy bits' for my audience? (See Chapter 6.)
- How do I need to frame the topic?
- What else can I do to get this audience to relate to the topic?

2. The audience on you

As with a topic, any audience will hold a range of assumptions about you as a speaker. You have done it many times before towards other speakers, so don't worry, it's nothing personal. Read down this list of speakers to see the different reactions they can evoke, from 'Wow!' to 'Who?' to 'Eugh':

- Tony Robbins
- Hillary Clinton
- Tanni Grey-Thompson
- Ken Robinson
- Marianne Williamson
- Stephen Hawking.

These are all speakers in the public eye, but the audience will apply similar judgement to you as a speaker. From the second you stand up to the moment you sit down, you give out signals about who you are as a speaker, what you stand for and what you will give to the audience. We looked at how your body and voice affect this in Part 1; now let's look at how you can empathise with the hopes your audience have about you as a speaker.

Exactly the same speech can be delivered in countless different ways by different speakers, depending on the personal touch they bring. What will be your personal touch? How can you make sure it's the best one for empathising with your audience?

Ask yourself the following questions to get into your audience's mindset:

- What does my audience know about me?
- What will they assume about me because of what they already know?
- What would they ideally like me to do or say?
- What would they not like me to do or say?
- What would surprise or delight my audience about my performance?

These questions will point you towards your audience's hopes for you as their speaker. Now, map out their hopes on the diagram below to help you consider how best to empathise with them.

1 'I expect a lot from this speaker'

'I don't expect much from this speaker'

2 'Make me laugh'

'Give it to me straight'

3 'I'm looking for information'

'I'm looking for inspiration'

1. 'I expect a lot' vs 'I don't expect much from this speaker'

Even if you are not a public speaker, your audience will hold hopes for you based on what they know about you. This could be as abstract as 'Oh, she's wearing a bright green dress, this might be interesting', or as detailed as 'I've known Jimmy for 12 years and he's always the one to make a joke in the room, he should be great'. Or it could be the organisation or social group you're associated with that builds or crushes your reputation by proxy – 'He's from Amnesty, I love what they do,' or 'Uff, not another local government officer, do I really have to be here?'

If you have presented a few times or more, don't be surprised that word gets round. It's easy to develop a reputation as a very good speaker, just as it's easy to develop a reputation as a speaker who should be avoided at all costs. Your reputation will decide where the bar of your audience's hopes for you is set. If you've set the bar high in previous encounters, the audience will hope for the same again. Make sure you don't disappoint, by always striving to give all you can to your audience. If you've set the bar low, you may have just a few moments at the beginning of your talk to recapture their enthusiasm, before they switch off.

Your analysis of your reputation will reveal how you should deliver your speech or presentation. When you start your talk, think about how much you need to say to introduce yourself. What information will help you gain credibility? You can raise the hopes of your audience, or modestly lower them, by the right choice of words at the beginning.

> ## What if . . . my audience don't like me?
>
> *Expert tip: Nigel Risner*
>
> Business coach, motivational speaker and author of *It's a Zoo Around Here*,[14] Nigel Risner says that if you're worried about your audience liking you, always make sure you've got a great opening line. He says: 'Most people panic on their first line and start with the same meaningless waffle as everyone else: "Hello, thank you very much, my name's Nigel and it's a pleasure to be here."[15]
>
> 'Get your audience on board with your first line and you're sorted. I often start with the question, "How many people in this room would like to have at least 5% more success in some part of their life?", which starts my talk off on a "Yes". Find an opening line that guarantees a "Yes" answer from 90% of your audience and half of the battle is won.
>
> 'Remember that in most speaking situations, 95% of the audience want to love you, they're on your side. The remaining 5% don't care how brilliant you are, they'll never like you. In every audience I speak to, 5% want to marry me, 5% want to kill me – it's bizarre. Acknowledge that this is all part of the game and focus on the 95% who like you.'

2. 'Make me laugh' vs 'Give it to me straight'

Are you delivering a speech, a toast or a workshop? Are you likely to have reverent faces staring at you, or are your audience clutching glasses of champagne and waiting to be entertained? The occasion, combined with your knowledge about your audience's other needs and expectations, will point to how much humour your audience are likely to be hoping for in your performance.

In many public speaking situations an audience will prefer to be made to laugh, even if it's gentle, reflective humour at a funeral. Humour can be used to defuse a tense situation, to build a sense of group cohesion, or to entertain. On some occasions, however, humour will be perceived in a negative light by an audience. Imagine an air hostess cracking a joke about flight safety, or a royal poking fun at the ambassador in front of a large audience. There's a time and a place to make the audience laugh and it's up to you to both judge what your audience is likely to hope for and to read the room as you're speaking. See Chapter 6 for more on humour.

3. Information vs inspiration

In some situations such as a lecture, a business meeting or an announcement, you have crucial information to deliver. Here, *what* you say is more important than *how* you say it. On other occasions, such as toasts and speeches, it's the inspiration you leave the audience with that is more important than the specifics of the content of your speech.

Speakers use all sorts of tools – photos, videos, interactive games, props, acting, etc. – to get across their message (more on these tools later, in Chapters 6, 7 and 9), but it's up to you to choose the balance wisely to build the maximum amount of empathy with your audience.

If your talk is factual, use these tools to support and re-emphasise your factual message. Just because you have a factual message doesn't mean that this must translate into a generic PowerPoint presentation. Ask yourself what your audience really want from a factual speech or presentation. They are probably looking for 'Aha!' moments where they understand the topic more effectively, or have learned a new way of applying it to themselves. How can you as a speaker maximise the chance of 'Aha!'?

If your audience are hoping for an emotional delivery, step up and give them as much as you have. Support your delivery with photographs, videos and other media that evoke the appropriate emotion. Audiences with these hopes love to see their speaker being deeply honest, so soul-search a little to find a touching and authentic way to deliver your message. For example, a groom could spend 15 minutes telling his wedding party how happy he is that he has married Sophie. Or he could say nothing and instead, with the audience focused on him, slowly and delicately pull out a tiny pair of baby socks to give to his new wife. Which do you think would best empathise with the group's needs?

4. Just how I like it

Other hopes the audience may have of you relate to the way you manage a speaking engagement. These include the length of speech – 'Keep it short and sweet' vs 'You should be thorough' – and the amount of audience involvement – 'I just want to listen' vs 'I want to be involved'.

The audience may not consciously be aware of their own hopes, so it's up to you to figure out what would really go down well for your listeners, based on everything else you know about them. If they're likely to be an impatient audience, get through your material succinctly, then give them a chance to ask questions (if appropriate). If your audience have that 'first day of term' enthusiasm, you might increase the amount of content you put in. If they are a quiet or nervous audience, expect either to have to talk more or to make more effort to get them involved. Again, have a plan, but be ready to change it.

The audience on you

Putting the picture together

Now you know more about what your audience want from you, you can take some more decisions about how to speak:

- How do my audience want me to be as a speaker?
- How do they want me to relate to my material?
- How much humour should I be using?
- Should I focus on information or emotions?

3. The audience on the audience

Finally, it's worth briefly mentioning the needs that come from how the audience view themselves, as individuals and as a group. Imagine you were in the following group situations. How would you feel? How would you react to the other members of your group? What would you need from the speaker to help you make the most of their public speaking?

- Listening to a church sermon.
- You, the adult, listening to the teacher along with a classroom of six year olds.

- Participating in a pitch at a sales meeting.
- Watching a comedian at the Hammersmith Apollo.
- Sitting in a large conference room listening to a speaker who fascinates you.

Perhaps as a member of a congregation you'd want your faith or lack of faith to be recognised. Perhaps as an adult in the classroom you'd like the teacher to treat you differently to the six year olds. And perhaps while watching a comedian you'd desperately like to stay anonymous, rather than become the butt of his jokes. These needs may be shared by other members of the audience, but not necessarily all of them. Here it is important to start noticing common threads that run through all or different parts of your audience.

Get under the skin of your audience. As individuals, do they secretly yearn to be recognised as intelligent? Important? Are they nervous, but want to feel confident? Do they long to be seen as good at what they do? Do they see themselves as party animals? Good, honest people? How many of them feel lonely or isolated in the room? Choose the characteristics your audience would be most likely to associate with and be sure to talk to them as if they already possess these qualities. This is a sure way of pushing their empathy buttons. Here are a few ideas of how that might look.

An audience needing to be recognised as 'good, honest people'

I can see we all care deeply about this. And the spirit of understanding within this room is deeply impressive.

NB: the repetition of 'deeply' acknowledges the depth or maturity of the audience.

An audience needing to be recognised as confident

As I walked into this room, I felt an air of expectation. 'Can I make it through this year?' 'Is it going to be as difficult as everyone says?' Well. I know that you can do it. You know you can do it. We know that we can do it.

NB: Positive language and the repetition of 'can do it' builds confidence.

An audience with a high number of people feeling lonely

We all know how daunting a new environment can be. Take a look around you at all the new and diverse faces in the room. There's so much to learn from each other. Now, catch someone by the eye, shake their hand and tell them, 'Well done for being here'.

> NB: this example skilfully draws together lonely members of the group and gives them an 'ice-breaking' connection to another audience member.

The audience on the audience

Putting the picture together

Based on the audience's image of themselves and as a group, ask yourself:

- What language should I use to relate to the audience?
- What do they want me to see in them as individuals, or as a group?
- What sort of ice-breaking activities are needed?
- How will the group respond to interactive exercises?

Setting up your environment

The next part of developing empathy is to understand how the environment in which you're speaking affects the audience. As a speaker, you're often in charge of how you manage your room to get the most out of it. Don't assume that because a room is set up in a certain way you have to stick to it. So long as you arrive at the room in advance, there are usually a number of things you can do to set up shop in a way that will best suit the needs of your audience.

Layout

You can see the power of room layout by comparing the House of Commons with a theatre such as Shakespeare's Globe. The Commons, with its two 'audiences' facing each other, encourages participation from all, whereas the Globe focuses everyone's attention on the stage and asks the audience to listen.

Consider how your room layout affects your message and change it if necessary. Here are some ideas:

- If you want your workshop group to feel more together, connect the ends of your horseshoe to make a circle.
- For a theatre setup that signals 'dynamic' to the audience, curve in some of the chairs at the front to be more surrounded by the audience.
- Deliberately change the end you'll speak from in your boardroom to show the audience 'we're going to think differently now'. You'll be surprised how different it feels for the audience to be looking at a new piece of wall. It feels like breaking the rules and they'll love you for it!
- Instead of standing at the top table, why not move through your audience as you speak to a cabaret-style room? Microphone permitting, this could be a good way to satisfy the audience's hopes to connect with their speaker.

Sitting in their seats

Even if you have an event manager organising your speaking engagement, take responsibility for your audience's experience by checking some environmental factors that are critical to their enjoyment. Start by sitting in a few of the seats the audience will occupy and ask yourself some questions from their point of view:

- **What can I see?** Are there any distractions that will take the audience's attention away from you? Windows, moving objects, or interesting things to read behind your stage may pull attention away from you while you're speaking.

- **What does the setup say about the speaker?** You can reinforce your key messages by placing relevant props or visual aids on stage for the audience to see as they come into the room. Many speakers use presentation banners, but equally you could use a model skeleton, a flag, or a mop and brush as part of your stage setup – whatever would link with your message. Props are a great idea if your audience are open to a bit of fun.

- **How comfortable is it to sit here?** Is the room too hot or too cold? Conference delegates often sit shivering in rooms with air conditioning, when the speaker could easily put them out of their misery by having it turned down.

- **What other noises, quirks of the room or other environmental factors do I notice?** Pick up these small pieces of information so that when you're speaking you can relate to and refer to what your audience are experiencing, rather than to your own environment on stage, which will be very different. A quick comment like 'Oof, it's cold in here – I'm afraid the heating's broken, so we'll all have to battle through' will show your audience that you empathise with their needs.

Chapter

Key wisdom from this chapter

- **Love thy audience:** if you think negatively of your audience, you'll be surrounded by difficult, aggressive listeners. If you seek to love them, you'll start to notice that they may be nervous, curious, tired or worried – and that you can help them.

- **Set agreements with your audience:** show them at the start what to expect and they're more likely to enjoy your talk.

- **Manage any difficult audience types:** find ways to engage or neutralise difficult audience types. Typically, through being authentic and seeking to serve them, you can win over any audience member. And if you can't, it's probably their issue, not yours.

- **Build an ongoing relationship by seeking feedback:** your audience are the best mentors to help your public speaking to improve in the long term. Ask them for suggestions for what you could do better and listen to the critique without taking it personally.

Managing the crowd

You've prepared by developing bundles of empathy with who you *think* your audience are, so now you're ready to face them. But how do you stay connected to your audience throughout the talk?

Love thy audience

As you start your speaking, check your attitude towards your audience. Do you love them and wish to serve them, or do you secretly see them as an inconvenience? When we notice ourselves feeling negative towards the audience, it's usually a signal that we're in the mindset of the egocentric speaker.

When we feel negative or defensive towards our audience, we might:

- become negative, defensive or aggressive as a reaction
- put on a 'mask' that dents our authenticity
- become tense or lose our connection with other members of the audience
- judge ourselves as failing
- find speaking difficult or awkward.

Check for yourself: do you perceive your audience as the top or the bottom line?

If you shift your attitude to that of the servant speaker, you give yourself space to think more positive and more useful thoughts about your audience. You start to focus on their potential and their needs rather than on your self-doubt. This will in turn improve your performance in speaking as your audience will see that you're trying to help them. This attitude is critical when handling tricky audience types, like the ones described later in this chapter.

Before you start your talk, set the intention to 'love thy audience' and benefit them in whatever way you can.

Setting agreements with your audience

You've set your attitude and now you start speaking. The first few minutes of your talk are crucial for getting your audience on your side. Here, try to introduce your topic and connect it to your audience so that they're ready to go on a journey with you. This is the first part of the hero's journey, which we'll look into in Part 3.

Use your empathetic preparation to tell you what your audience need you to clarify or 'put in the room' before you leap into your content. Remember to voice any agreements that need to be made around:

- what they should expect from the **topic:**
  - what's important about the topic
  - what you are going to talk about

THE AUDIENCE AS AN ANNOYANCE...

KNOW-IT-ALL

EAGER TO PLEASE YOU

RUDE

TRYING TO HIDE HER NERVES

TROUBLE

EXCITED ABOUT WHAT YOU'RE SAYING

- what they should expect from you as the **speaker**:
  - what is your area of expertise
  - how much time you are likely to spend
  - what style you will use
- you recognising who they are and what they need as an **audience**.

Here's how you might quickly come to agreement with your audience.

1. Show the audience what you know about them

We have an élite in this room. Renowned doctors, lawyers and scientists [agreement for an audience who need to be seen as intelligent]. *I'm really grateful for an hour of your time* [agreement on time]. *I've*

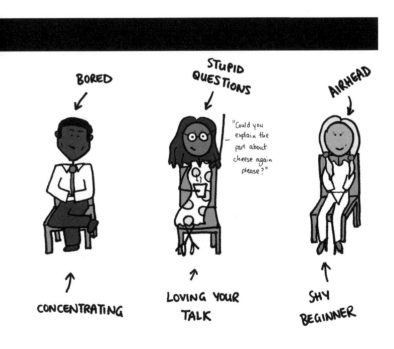

already had a lot of questions from you about my topic, so I'm honoured to be presenting you with information that's both current and relevant to your work [agreement on topic]. *In this talk I'll summarise my department's latest research for you* [agreement on speaker's expertise]. *And because we're all busy people, my guess is that you'd appreciate as much information as possible from me in the time we have together* [agreement on speaker style – 'I'll give lots of information'].

2. Check that this is true

Does this sound good to you? If you receive a resounding 'Yes!', move down to point three. If it doesn't come, or you sense from the audience that they were hoping for something else, adjust your agreement with them: *No problem, it looks like some of you have different hopes from me. I want you all to leave here with what you came for, so I'll be sure to leave a good length of time at the end for your questions.*

Or: *I don't see many nods – is there something else you wanted from this talk?*

3. Once you have an agreement, show them how you've tailored what you're going to say to their specific needs

Great, let's jump in. Those of you who have seen me speaking before will know that I like to use video clips in my presentations [agreement on speaker style] *so let's kick off with this one ...*

Or: *Ok. I know that we learn best by doing and reflecting, so let me start by asking you a question.*

Different audience types and how to handle them

As you continue through your speech, different audience personalities may emerge, with different needs. Back in 1970 Richard Mann and his colleagues[16] created a model of eight different audience types a teacher experiences in a college classroom. Below is my reworking of their brilliant model (which has seven types) to help you get an understanding of the different characters you might experience in an audience and how best to serve them.

1. The sheep

- Sheep are conventional, focused on what you're saying and look to you for the answers. They rarely question your control.

- They listen hoping to understand the material and often prefer a lecture to a discussion. Sheep speak out only to agree or to ask clarifying questions.

- Sheep are unlikely to show independence or creativity. They might find creative questions and tasks more difficult than others, so clear instructions are important.

If you have a room full of sheep: you'll get the feeling of being rather important, just like a shepherd to a flock. You will notice an atmosphere of respect and perhaps reverence. This is common in large, adult audiences, where there is a high level of desire to hear what you have to say. Don't worry if eye contact is limited, it's probably because your fluffy white sheep are busy taking notes.

How to handle sheep: sheep will feel like your allies. You can also use them to chip in on your side if you're asked a difficult or negative question. If you're struggling with holding an audience it could be because you lack sheep. Turn other audience types into compliant sheep by illustrating what you and the audience have in common. Keep them following you by demonstrating your authenticity – for example, don't pretend to know the answer to a question if you don't know. If sheep pick up on the vibes of inauthenticity, they'll stop trusting you and wander off elsewhere. If you want to stimulate your sheep into a more active role, encourage them to make critical comments and to contribute to discussions.

2. The hotshot

Hotshots are comfortable and confident members of the audience, often with high status in that social group.

- They listen intently to what you have to offer, while at the same time keeping in mind their own learning goals.

- They love seminar or discussion formats and are high-level participators.

- They easily make friends or enemies with the speaker depending on how much they trust you.
- They learn quickly and will ask challenging questions to deepen their learning or to clarify their understanding.
- If you're not performing as the audience hoped and there is the time and social dynamic to make a complaint or suggestion, hotshots will often act as spokesperson for the group's concerns.

If you have a room full of hotshots: your audience will seem engaged, participative, positive and challenging. Discussions will flow easily and insightful comments will arise naturally. An audience like this will quickly know if you are confident in your topic or haven't prepared enough.

How to handle hotshots: prepare your topic well. Acknowledge their independence – 'I can tell you've thought a lot about this subject and thank you for that' – and encourage them to push beyond what is expected of other audience types. Focus on delivering unusual insights that deepen their understanding of the topic. Back up your arguments with evidence. If you don't know the answer to their question, don't fake it. Tell them it's a good question and either take it offline ('Speak to me about it after'), say you'll find out for them (and make sure you do) or bounce it back to the audience ('Honestly, I don't know. Can anyone in the audience help?' or 'What do you think?'). Hotshots will be keen to soak up your information, so make them aware if handouts are coming at the end, or allow them the time to note down key points.

3. The clown

- Clowns love the social part of listening to a public speaker and this is often more important to them than absorbing information.
- They're chatty and often offer lively comments and questions to entertain rather than to support the speaker.
- Clowns love discussion and interactive exercises and are often the most socially outgoing in group activities.
- If treated well, clowns are pleasant to have in an audience and are capable of focusing well if they see others concentrating.
- Clowns are easy to motivate by giving them attention.

If you have a room full of clowns: there will be a bubbly, lively atmosphere, but the feel will be different from a room full of hotshots. Here you will face more audience comments, laughter and perhaps in-conversations. This can result in anything from fun to frustration, depending on how you manage your clowns.

How to handle clowns: they love to be entertained, so tell them a good story, or express yourself with passion. Avoid being too serious with them or you'll seem pompous. Bring laughter and allow your clowns to enjoy it, but be careful to keep the focus on your topic throughout. If you need clowns to be calmer or more serious, bring your talk back to its key purpose and the deeper meaning of it. Think what the audience really care about and remind them of it.

Clowns are socially confident, so they're the ones to turn to if you want participation from the group. Encourage them to speak, but be careful to keep them on track. Don't let them take over – you are still the speaker.

Also, make sure you avoid getting distracted from other audience types just because your clowns are entertaining and noisy. Channel their energy to contribute towards your message.

Audience types: the sheep, the sniper and the black cloud

4. The sniper

- Snipers start out with a hostile or cynical attitude towards you or your topic.
- They are often switched on and listening out for an opportunity to criticise or show their expertise in the room.
- They have strong attention spans and can be used well for discussions where critical analysis is important.
- This is often the person you fear in question and answer sessions. Don't let the sniper take over the room with their questions and don't forget they are typically just one person.

If you have a room full of snipers: you'll notice an atmosphere of competition and aggression, individuals trying to win a point or show themselves to be the most intelligent. Arms may be folded or eyes rolled as you start to speak. Preparation and confidence are very important when handling this audience type.

How to handle snipers: first of all, recognise your expertise – you are standing at the front of the room for a reason. Snipers are a problem only if you're feeling uncomfortable – otherwise they can't hurt you. Although snipers may sound personal, remember that the sniper doesn't want to cause you pain, they want an answer to their question. Love thy audience! Avoid taking their bullet yourself by directing the sniper back to the topic in hand, to see if the sniper's view of the world is legitimate. It may well be. Refer to the topic as 'ours', so that you are discussing rather than defending your standpoint.

Speaker [jovially]: *As we've all experienced, alcohol is usually needed before British gentlemen are able to express their emotions!*

Sniper [angrily]: *Yes, but you're wrong, aren't you? I proposed to my wife sober. I talk emotionally to her all the time. I don't even drink.*

Speaker [calmly]: *Thanks for sharing.* [To the whole audience] *What do you think? Does that make our rule invalid, or is it the exception that proves the rule?*

Welcome the comments rather than battling them or you will only stoke the sniper's fire. Resist the temptation to try to 'win' the argument. Provide reasonable and tangible evidence to support your point and leave it at that. Often snipers' energy will fizzle out if they are left unprovoked.

5. The snowman

- No matter how much you talk to a snowman (in real life or in your audience), they won't respond. Snowmen are habitually quiet and may seem disconnected or bored in an audience.
- They are unlikely to respond if you ask a question, but will usually be paying close attention to the details of your talk.

What if . . . an audience member is really rude to me?

Expert tip: Nick Williams

'Harsh feedback cannot always be avoided' says best-selling author and speaker Nick Williams,[17] who has 20 years' experience inspiring entrepreneurs. But don't let the fear of that stop you doing anything. If rudeness comes your way, he suggests:

1 Don't take it too personally – you may well have hit someone's emotional hot button – but it is *their* hot button, not yours. Allow them to have their thoughts and feelings.

2 Be aware of your own emotional hot buttons – judgement or criticism can lead you to feel hurt, angry or defensive. Don't resist this, but be willing to explore those feelings and develop ways of 'desensitising' yourself.

3 Anticipate what you fear – think through the questions, statements or challenges you might dread getting thrown at you and imagine what you'd say, how you'd feel and what you'd think in response. By preparing you feel more confident and less defensive.

'Many of my hot buttons have been triggered over the years, and my goal is to use them as great self-awareness and giving me insights into places where I need to do some inner work so I am less defensive and more open. Over time, I have aimed to develop my character, rather than use clever tips or techniques – it seems to have worked for me.

'Never forget that having an audience listen to you is a great honour and we should treat it as such.'

- Snowmen often secretly desire a close relationship with the speaker, but are afraid because the speaker seems more important than them.

- Snowmen are often found in technical specialities and professions where human contact is infrequent or unimportant. They may also become a snowman around your topic if they feel lacking in confidence in that area.

If you have a room full of snowmen: you'll notice that it's very difficult to get a reaction from them – questions and interactive exercises will feel laboured. Eye contact and reassuring smiles may be limited as snowmen don't imagine the speaker needs their support.

How to handle snowmen: the biggest mistake you can make is to ignore the snowmen. As I've mentioned before, it's important to make sure every participant receives attention. Do this by smiling at individuals, walking to their part of the room, making eye contact and so on. Create a welcoming atmosphere and they'll engage with your topic in the way that best benefits them.

If you want to interact with them, start with interactivity that's within their comfort zone – e.g. a 'pair share' (see Chapter 10). Snowmen are often the most reflective members of an audience. Because of their detachment from the group they can offer useful insights into the topic if you ask them directly for their opinion.

6. The black cloud

- The black cloud is characterised by negative body language, such as frowning, wandering eyes, folded arms or slumped shoulders. Take care when judging this audience type because an audience member who is frowning may just be concentrating hard.
- Black clouds hold a resigned, 'can't do' attitude to themselves with respect to the subject matter. They believe it is a tricky, boring or irrelevant subject.
- They take more energy to motivate than others and are easily bored.
- Turned off by typical ways of presenting, the black cloud has probably 'seen it all before' and decided they don't like it or can't do it.
- Black clouds can also be other audience types who, after a long day of listening to unimpressive speakers, are tired of listening.

If you have a room full of black clouds: you'll notice low energy, slumped body language and low resonance with what you're saying. Black clouds will have a glazed look in their eyes – provided they haven't just been watching something interesting on YouTube.

How to handle black clouds: start by explaining the ways in which your message differs in style or method of delivery from the usual explanation on the matter. If your room is full of black clouds, get some energy flowing with movement or interactivity, taking care to explain why you're doing it – 'We're going to have some interesting discussions today, so let's first get to know each other better by playing a short game.'

Bring some sunshine to your black clouds by showing extra enthusiasm towards your subject so that they get carried along. If you drop down to their energy level, everyone will leave the room depressed.

Recognise that the subject may be difficult for them and offer reassurance that you can change that for them. Once they are on board, compliment and encourage the black cloud on any input they give to a session. Offer them supportive and energetic gestures and eye contact to show that the subject matter isn't as deadly serious as they may have thought.

7. The unwanted panellist

- This is the 'expert' in the room who hasn't been asked to present.
- Similar to the clown, the unwanted panellist has a high degree of confidence but they lack respect for, or awareness of, the social protocol expected in the group.
- The unwanted panellist will frequently try to add to your knowledge by attempting to teach the audience from their own experience. This can sometimes be a deliberate attempt to win business or respect from the audience.
- They might ask you a 'question' which is really a statement designed to show that their knowledge is greater than yours.
- It's easy to become irritated by the unwanted panellist, but remember that other members of the audience also see them as irritating, pushy or distracting.

If you have a room full of unwanted panellists: there's usually only space for a couple of unwanted panellists in the room. But if there are more, your talk or workshop will feel really out of control, with people chipping in with competing stories and ideas all over the place. Unwanted panellists create friction with audience members who came to hear you speak, so it's up to you to minimise the disturbance they cause.

How to handle the unwanted panellist: ideally you should have no unwanted panellists in the room – they should either stay silent or speak when appropriate. To help this happen, build the right agreements before you start the main body of your talk. Try agreements like 'Let's come to this room with an open mind and leave whatever outside knowledge and experience we have outside the door', or 'I'm going to give you my approach to this subject. Hear me out and then if you'd like to challenge me at the end I'll leave time for a bit of debate.'

If your unwanted panellist continues to perk up, judge what the rest of your audience need. If they're causing prickles of frustration, remind them that you are the speaker in the room and that if they have more to say you'd be happy to discuss it afterwards. Speak firmly but calmly and your audience will thank you for it.

Ultimately, audiences are more likely to get difficult when they can sense that:

1. **You're not being authentic:** if you're not acting like a human being, why should they treat you as such?
2. **You've forgotten about them:** if you're not being empathetic to their needs, why would you expect them to be empathetic towards you?
3. **You haven't prepared enough:** if you haven't given enough respect to your public speaking, why should they?

These three mistakes are surprisingly common in public speaking. Each of them is easily solved if you remember the six qualities of an inspiring speaker: authenticity, empathy, balance, freshness, fearlessness and awareness. If you allow all six qualities to flourish in your speaking, most audience difficulties will disappear. Then, if an audience member is *still* difficult, the chances are it's their issue, not yours. If that's the case, you can just let it go.

What if . . . I get an awkward question from my audience?

Expert tip: Mamta Saha

'Mindset is very important when answering awkward questions,' says psychologist Mamta Saha[18] from Think Spa. 'You have to believe the audience are on your side. Before you speak, tell yourself that any questions you get from the audience are coming from a place of "wanting to understand" your content, not from wanting to trip you up.

'If you are already dreading the thought of people asking you questions before you speak, you naturally create an uncomfortable anxiousness in yourself and the audience, who will be quick to pick up and respond to this anxiety. If you stay calm and approach questions in a positive way, you keep your audience engaged and maintain your confidence throughout.

'When an awkward question is asked, summarise it to yourself in your mind and then repeat it back to the audience in your own words. This shows that you "hear" what they are saying and allows you to check your understanding. In the meantime, you have a little space to process the question. You are then in a position to share your insights on the question, form an opinion and share your thoughts.

'If you still need more time, you might say, "This is a very interesting stance", or "I haven't heard that point of view before", which gives you an opportunity to open the question up to the audience. You could go on to invite the audience to comment: "Does anyone in the room have experience of this?" or "Let me think about that – any suggestions from the audience?" As they speak, you will find your own expertise to add.'

Holding empathy with your audience beyond your performance

If you would like to have an ongoing relationship with your audience, holding empathy beyond the room where you spoke is crucial. Here's how.

1. Invite feedback

If you've delivered a long talk or workshop, get the audience to complete an evaluation form. Here are five key feedback questions to ask, which will help you understand how you did – and how to understand your audience better for next time:

1. What was your experience of the topic before you came to this workshop?
2. How do you feel about this topic now?
3. What was your key takeaway from the talk?
4. Which parts were less relevant to you?
5. What would help you to take more from this talk? (Please comment on the speaker and/or the content.)

Then take away the feedback and look at it from an impersonal standpoint. Avoid getting caught up on any feedback that's too positive or too negative. Look at what you can do next time to better serve your audience.

2. The aftermath

- Stick around after you've finished speaking to answer any questions. If you have a crowd battling to speak to you, well done – you've hit a nerve with them.
- Remember that authentic speakers are the same on-stage and off-stage. If you are bubbly and friendly when speaking but scowl at an audience member 'I'm busy' as you leave the room, you will break the good feeling you built up while you were talking.

3. Follow up

- Follow up on anything you've promised to do during your talk. It's easy to let things slide when the adrenaline of speaking is gone, but following up your commitments will show the audience that you're trustworthy. Even if you never see that audience member again, they will spread the word that you are a speaker to be trusted.
- Where appropriate, be sure to get the contact details of your audience members and follow up with an email, a thank you or a resource from your talk. This is especially important when you're hoping to generate business from speaking.

Part

3

If you can't write your message in a sentence,
you can't say it in an hour.

Dianna Booher

Lucy Longtalk glanced at her audience and frowned. 'Why are they fidgeting so much?' she asked herself.

They had been so enthusiastic when she'd started talking. The audience had been brimming with energy at the beginning and there was even a moment where the whole group had clapped at something she'd said. But now, 55 minutes later, they had glazed looks on their faces and a couple of them were even checking their phones as she was speaking.

'It's like a completely different audience,' Lucy thought. 'What's gone wrong?'

Balance

In Part 3:

- Lessons from TED Talks on structuring a powerful speech.

- How to identify one idea worth spreading to frame your talk around.

- A test for your ideas that will make sure you fascinate your audience.

- The journey method for structuring a talk.

- Powerful tools for editing a talk – to weed out the excess and highlight your key messages.

You've used awareness to master your nervous quirks and you've figured out what to say by empathetically focusing on your audience. Now it's time to decide which content goes where.

This is where otherwise brilliant public speakers get tripped up. They talk for too long. They put too much emphasis on one area to the detriment of the rest of their talk. They put in too many facts, or not enough. They try to fit too much in. Part 3 is all about getting the balance right.

Balance what?

Balance is all about negotiating which information goes in and which stays out to have the maximum power in your speaking. Some of the key negotiations in your content are shown in the table.

Authenticity: sticking up for the message I deeply wish to share, even at the risk of breaking rapport	vs	**Empathy:** resonating with my audience's aims, desires and fears about my subject
Facts: emphasising credibility and logical evidence	vs	**Feeling:** emphasising *felt* experience and emotions
Telling: asserting your message	vs	**Asking:** eliciting an answer from the group
Minimalist language: a clear, stark message	vs	**Elaborate language:** using rich, descriptive words to evoke the senses
Clarity: easy to follow and simple, perhaps 'high level' with minimal jargon, great for beginners	vs	**Depth:** the complete detail or background to an argument. Enough depth for the experts

What is the right balance for your topic on each of these contrasts?

What is perfect balance?

We can feel when a talk has balance. It will feel like the simplest, easiest talk in the world to listen to. It will feel intuitively correct in its rhythm and narrative. But simplicity can be deceptive – usually that speaker has battled through many layers of complexity to develop a place of clarity.

Balance is:

- the sensitivity to be able to judge which information goes where in a talk
- creating a journey for your audience that keeps them engaged throughout
- choosing a theme or idea that threads through the whole talk, offering a pathway to return to
- ordering your flow of information so that the audience leave with your key points in their minds
- creating compelling structures that help you – and your audience – remember your words.

How do you develop balanced structure?

We'll look at two key aspects of a talk that help you to create balance:

1. **Compelling concept:** we'll take inspiration from TED Talks to identify the thread that runs through your entire talk.
2. **Structure and the hero's journey:** using classic storytelling structures to organise your content into a compelling journey.

Chapter

Key wisdom from this chapter

- **Find your 'idea worth spreading':** the best talks are framed around one compelling idea, which is easy to understand yet highly insightful.

- **Look for your gourmet dish:** when picking your content, don't go for the all-you-can-eat buffet approach to cramming in information as this will give your audience indigestion! Instead, create one delicious dish that has memorable flavours.

- **Dream big with your talk concept:** look for an idea that really could change the world, or at least your audience's world. Be bold and idealistic and your talk will benefit.

- **Do the 'Ooh' test on your ideas:** as you test your talk content, look for the reaction of your friends or colleagues. A reaction of 'Oh, that's interesting' means there's more work to be done, but if you get an 'Ooh!', you're onto something.

Compelling content – lessons from TED

Finding my 'idea worth spreading'

As I've already mentioned, TED.com is an incredible platform for powerful short talks that has well and truly raised the bar for short talks and presentations. It is increasingly common for TED-style talks to be delivered at conferences and if you're hoping to attract attention to your business or project, there's plenty to learn from TED.

What is the TED format?

- TED originally stood for technology, entertainment and design, but speakers now cover wide-ranging subjects in a compelling and entertaining way.
- TED Talks are short talks of up to 18 minutes.
- In that time, speakers are encouraged to offer *one idea worth spreading* to their audience.

TED speakers are given the ten 'TED commandments' to shape their talk. The most common (and I think most accessible) version of this is below:

1. **Dream big:** strive to create the best talk you have ever given. Reveal something never seen before. Do something the audience will remember for ever. Share an idea that could change the world.
2. **Show us the real you:** share your passions, your dreams . . . and also your fears. Be vulnerable. Speak of failure as well as success.
3. **Make the complex plain:** don't try to dazzle intellectually. Don't speak in abstractions. Explain! Give examples. Tell stories. Be specific.

4. **Connect with people's emotions:** make us laugh! Make us cry!

5. **Don't flaunt your ego:** don't boast. It's the surest way to switch everyone off.

6. **No selling from the stage!** Unless specifically asked, do not talk about your company or organisation. And don't even think about pitching your products or services or asking for funding from the stage.

7. **Feel free to comment on other speakers' talks, to praise or to criticise:** controversy energises. Enthusiastic endorsement is powerful.

8. **Don't read your talk:** notes are fine, but if the choice is between reading or rambling, then read!

9. **End your talk on time:** doing otherwise is to steal time from the people who follow you. We won't allow it.

10. **Rehearse your talk:** for timing, for clarity, for impact.

There is so much to learn from the TED style, but the single most important contribution these talks have made to public speaking is the emphasis on *one idea worth spreading*. This will revolutionise your speaking.

> ## Public speaking myth
>
> *Words don't matter*
>
> There is a commonly misquoted study by psychologist Albert Mehrabian[19] which says that communication is 55% body language, 38% tone of voice and 7% words. In reality, his study was about one-to-one communications where likes and dislikes were being expressed in one-word answers. Mehrabian has tried to express his displeasure at the misuse of his study, yet the myth persists.
>
> What's more, the numbers aren't even helpful. Try listening to a TED Talk with the sound turned off and see whether you understand 55% of the meaning through the body language of the speakers alone.

Only *one* idea?

Deciding on what to say in your talk is like going to a delicious buffet. You only have one plate, but you want to fill it with as many goodies as possible. That's better value, right?

So you start by putting on some seafood, a little pâté, salad, rice. Then you're putting on some steak, a sausage, macaroni and cheese, potato, salsa, caviar, omelette, curry, chicken wings . . . Your plate is full. Then you realise you've forgotten dessert – and not wanting to miss out, you squash it to the side of the sausage.

What you're left with is a combination of flavours that merges into one. You couldn't say afterwards what you ate. And you might just end up with indigestion. Isn't it like that for your audience sometimes?

What we're really looking for is one gourmet dish for the audience to savour – that's your *idea worth spreading*. If it's simple and delicious they are much more likely to talk about it afterwards.

Studies show that given too much choice, consumers pick nothing. The same goes for audience members. If they're given too many message options, they will remember less, not more.

How to find that one compelling concept

Know what you're looking for

Great talk concepts are:

- **Clear:** precisely what message would you like your audience to take away? If you don't know, spend some time clarifying this. Surprisingly few speakers ask themselves this question and then they wonder why their message doesn't get heard.

- **Simple:** as communications specialist Dianna Booher said,[20] 'If you can't write your message in a sentence, you can't say it in an hour.' What she meant is that as speakers we need to be able to hone our message into its core essence to make any sense of it at all.

- **Unique:** we remember ideas better if they are different to all the others we've heard. Be bold! One of my speakers, a climate change lecturer at a law school, came up with the idea, 'What if law did yoga? How would that impact climate change regulations?' This quirky and memorable idea was totally different to what her industry was used to hearing – and brought surprisingly powerful insights.

- **Useful:** the idea 'how to mash potato with your feet' might be clear, simple and unique, but unless it connects to something that benefits me as an audience member, it's not an idea worth spreading, it's an idea worth losing.

- **Edgy:** the most attention-grabbing ideas might be controversial, racy, ridiculous, emotive or provocative. In his brave TEDx talk,[21] Brian Goldman broke a long-standing taboo in the medical profession and told us, 'Doctors kill people. I've killed people. If we can talk about this, we can learn from our mistakes.'

Example 'ideas worth spreading' from five of my favourite TED Talks (available from www.ted.com)

- **Benjamin Zander:** we can all love classical music.
- **Jamie Oliver:** let's start a food revolution, starting with educating children about food.
- **Jill Bolte Taylor:** I had a stroke and discovered that there is deep and profound peace when you access the right side of your brain.
- **Simon Sinek:** great leaders start with *why* rather than with *what*.
- **Ken Robinson:** creativity is as important in education as literacy.

As TED suggest, dream big

Now you know the territory we're playing in, look at your topic and search for the biggest, most exciting idea. Don't censor yourself too soon, just brainstorm possible ideas and associations. This is a great way to come up with a new idea for a talk. Answer the questions below to stimulate your thinking:

A: If you have no idea what to talk about	B: If you want to jazz up your chosen topic
• What's your most outstanding personal or professional achievement?	• What's your big revelation that people don't know about? Or don't know *enough* about?
• What's an experience in your life that nobody else has?	• What does the world *just not get* about your topic?
• What do you know, think or suspect that nobody else does?	• If you were being rude and were 'telling me how it is', what would you say?
• What's your weirdest idea?	• Why on *earth* should I listen to YOU talk
• What's the most important thing in the world that you see needs to change?	about your topic? Go on, fight for it.
	• If I was a bit of an idiot, how would you explain your topic/message to me?
• What are you the guru of?	• What's urgent or current about your topic that I can connect to?
• What do you rant about in the pub with friends?	
• What would your best-selling book be titled?	• Take something completely unrelated – an animal, a sport, a movie, a machine, a job – and connect it to your topic.
• If you could dream up a change in the world, what would it be?	• Tell us a story!
• Tell us a story – then figure out what it could mean.	• What's funny about you, your life, or someone you know?

As you start thinking around your ideas, allow something new and innovative to develop. If it's too far out you can always drop it later. In fact, it takes fearlessness to come up with an idea worth spreading, so stick at it if it feels tough at the beginning.

Do the 'Ooh' test

When you have one or more ideas that you think might make a good talk concept, it's time to get some feedback. The problem with feedback is that unless you're asking an expert, prospective audience members will usually say, 'Oh yes, that sounds interesting', even if there's a much better angle you could take.

I suggest you use the 'Ooh' test. Tell your idea and wait for it to land. Then judge the reaction:

'Oh'	A simple 'oh' means your idea has well and truly failed to engage. Avoid!
'Ooh'	You have something that might engage, but it needs a bit more oomph.
'Oooh'	Looks like you've got a strong idea that engages the audience.
'Ooooooh!'	The longer the 'ooo', the more chance you're on to a winning concept that someone will talk about and share afterwards.

The more 'ooooh' you generate in your talk, the more memorable and pass-on-able your concept. This is how ideas can go from being more 'blah blah' in a sea of information to becoming game-changing concepts that make your reputation as an expert.

Chapter

8

Key wisdom from this chapter

- **Take your audience on a hero's journey:** the best talks make the audience feel like the heroes of the story – that they have had an adventure that's taught them something useful.

- **Use the opening to get them excited:** the opening is like the start of a mountain expedition. Quickly build trust and let them know which mountain you're climbing together.

- **Build the drama:** let the next thing you say be more interesting than the one before. That's how you stop a talk from sagging in the middle.

- **Close with power:** reach a climax in the logic or emotion of your talk and then wrap up quickly and powerfully.

- **Get out the editing scissors:** go through your talk and cut out any content that's weak in favour of bold, evocative and memorable words.

Structure and the hero's journey

Public speaking without a strong structure is like building a skyscraper out of jelly. If the form of your talk is slipping and wobbling about in front of you as you speak, if you're taking on-the-spot decisions about what information to put where, you will not construct the most effective message and will miss the opportunity to deliver it to your audience.

But remember, structure is not:

- **a set of shackles:** once you have devised your structure, it is not something that you have to stick to obsessively throughout your talk. As I mentioned earlier, it is often the moments when we go off-piste (either through a mistake or through our passion) that we seem more human and more likeable as a speaker. As you design your structure, keep that freedom in the back of your mind

- **personality outsourcing:** no matter how good your structure is, you'll still need to use your awareness, empathy and freshness qualities to have an impact

- **a formula:** every talk has a slightly different purpose, so there is no single 'winning formula' for your structure. If there were, audiences would quickly become bored of it and crave something innovative. Be creative with balance and find out what works for you to keep your audience engaged and inspired.

Structure is:

- **your personal assistant:** structure is a way of organising your thoughts before you speak, so that you don't have to do too much thinking and decision-making when you're on stage

- **your rock:** structure is a firm, centred base for you to rely on, so that you can innovate or improvise and still come back to your central points

- **your power:** by establishing your key moments in advance of speaking, you no longer need to conjure inspiration as you're speaking – you're simply following a plan in which you have confidence. When the decision's already been made internally, you stand the best chance of putting your full force behind a powerful moment.

The hero's journey

The best speeches, like the best stories and movies, take the audience on a journey. It could be that the talk takes us on a literal journey from, say, Cape Kennedy to the moon, a metaphorical journey from angst to peace, or an intellectual journey from no knowledge to a complete picture.

In his seminal work *The Hero with a Thousand Faces*,[22] Joseph Campbell mapped out the idea of the *hero's journey*, tracking 17 stages an archetypical hero will go through on their quest. This pattern can be applied to most stories, movies and plays, from *Star Wars* to *Cinderella*. If parts of the journey are missing, that's when we may feel that a story is incomplete.

The 17 steps are too complex for public speaking, so I have developed a simple model for structure that can be used to bring power to public speaking of any length – the journey method. I've developed talks of just one minute, through to my six-month Inspiring Speakers Programme using these principles.

The journey method

We're standing at the bottom of a mountain and we're going to climb it. What could be simpler? If you have this level of clarity about the journey you want to take your audience on, you are heading in direction of a balanced, compelling talk.

But it's easy to get lost on your journey – perhaps because you didn't know what mountain you were climbing in the first place (in which case, return to the previous chapter to clarify your talk concept), or because the route you're taking is so long or confused that people lose energy on the way. Let's investigate what's needed to engage people every step of the way.

Who is the hero?

Make the audience the hero of your talk. Even if you're telling a personal story, it's the audience's experience of your journey that matters. By making them the hero, you can see the struggles, difficulties and triumphs of the journey from their perspective.

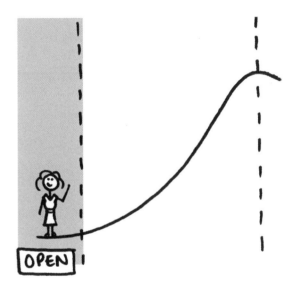

Part 1: The open (approx 10%)

Purpose:

1. Establish connection with your audience.
2. Set out the journey ahead.
3. Prepare them for the journey ahead.

Imagine you're a mountaineer taking a party up a mountain. The opening portion of a talk should include everything they need to know about you and about the journey to get going. This is where your empathetic preparation comes in most useful.

Your audience will want to know:

- **Why would I follow you?** I'd like to think my mountaineer has all the relevant certifications and experience to get me to the summit. Likewise, demonstrate your credibility during the opening. It's best if you can do this without boasting as that's a sure way to switch off an audience. Get someone else to introduce you, so they can praise your achievements and help the audience to see you as trustworthy.

- **Do you have a map?** We're not just wandering about the countryside, we're climbing a mountain. So your audience want to have a sense of where we're going from the very start. Even if we don't know the exact adventures we'll encounter on the way (audiences love surprises), we like to trust that you have a plan.

- **Why should I move? It's quite comfortable here, thanks.** The opening is also about setting up what's known in the hero's journey as the 'old story'. This is the hero's life before they went on an adventure that changed them, or it's the current situation in a topic that we're going to bring change around.

Here are some examples from speakers I've worked with:

Old story	Call to adventure
I was just a normal bloke who didn't like to stick out too much.	One day I was given such terrible news at work that I thought it would destroy everything ...
I've worked for two decades with quality managers within companies and they persistently ignore or excuse bad feedback.	I'm going to show you how to see that *bad news is good news* when getting feedback.
When it comes to numerous business scenarios like pay negotiations, women are still losing out in the workplace.	It was a shock for me to discover that men and women really *are* different and that if we treat them as such, our business benefits.
We imagine that in the Western world freedom is alive and well.	I thought so too, until a history student friend of mine went to Turkey to investigate the Armenian massacre – and never came back.

How important are opening lines?

In my experience, opening lines don't make or break a talk, but if you can open with power your audience will benefit much more than the usual throat-clearing, 'Hello, thanks so much for having me here, what a wonderful conference'. Here are some great TED Talk openers for inspiration:

- 'Imagine a big explosion as you climb through 3,000 feet. Imagine a plane full of smoke. Imagine an engine going clack, clack, clack, clack, clack, clack, clack. It sounds scary. Well, I had a unique seat that day. I was sitting in 1D.' **Ric Elias: 3 things I learned while my plane crashed**

- 'Sadly, in the next 18 minutes when I do our chat, four Americans that are alive will be dead from the food that they eat.' **Jamie Oliver: Teach every child about food**

- 'I'll tell you a little bit about irrational behaviour. Not yours, of course – other people's.' **Dan Ariely: Are we in control of our own decisions?**

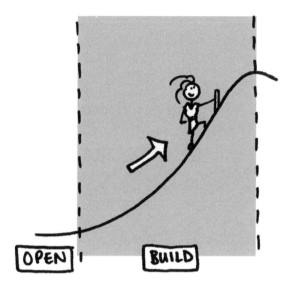

Part 2: The build (approx 80%)

Purpose:

1. Develop an argument or story.

2. Keep the audience interested the whole way by using dramatic contrast.

3. Reach a climax where your *idea worth spreading* is most powerfully evidenced.

We're heading up our mountain, but let's not make it too easy for the group to get there, otherwise we'll value it less when we reach the top. If you think about the story of Edmund Hillary climbing Everest for the first time, what keeps you listening are moments of drama and difficulty along the way. Aim to give your audience an exciting ride to keep them listening – this is known as the 'road of trials' in the hero's journey. This means:

- **Your next point should be more interesting than the one before.** This is the opposite of what many blogs or books do, putting their best content first. But if you want people to listen to your whole talk, keep back the most unusual, dramatic or convincing points until later in your talk.

  One client of mine started his talk about 'taking off the masks' by coming out to his wife as gay. The next story he wanted to tell was one of him at a networking event being too nervous to speak with anyone. While the stories were in chronological order, the first was such a big attention grabber for me that it either needed to be much further along the journey, or he needed something big to top it.

- **Don't try too much.** In a talk of about 20 minutes you can tell perhaps 3 stories with power. Don't forget that you're creating a gourmet meal, not loading the plate at a buffet.

- **Make it memorable.** Use every tool at your disposal to hold the audience's attention. We'll look at these in depth in Part 4.

- **Signpost the way.** Signal to your audience where you're at in the talk, e.g. 'Now to the fifth of our seven habits', or remind them of the key message, 'All the while I was wondering: how can we eradicate poverty in Mexico?' Signposts keep us on track, so that even if an audience member has wandered off to take a picture we can still follow the group up the mountain.

- **Carry themes and language through your talk.** The language you choose is critical for emphasising a clear journey. Let's say your talk is on creativity. Keep the word *creativity* coming back at regular intervals throughout your talk, rather than changing it to *innovation, thinking differently, blue sky thinking* and so on. Own your language.

- **Find your good versus evil.** Dramatic tension is built and maintained through contrasts, the most archetypical of which is 'good' versus 'evil'. Your 'evil' might relate to your *old story* – it's what you want to change, or the force that stops that change from happening. The 'good' is the alternative new world you're proposing, or a way to reach it. Some examples might be:

> Our department is *disorganised* (evil) vs Let's find *simplicity* (good).

> The *city* is manically *busy* (evil), let's find time to find *stillness* in *nature* (good).

> Fear made me *paralysed* (evil), but what I wanted was *freedom* (good).

> I have a *dream* (good), but there are people trying to *oppress* us (evil).

- **Look for a rhythm.** Powerful talks often contain a pattern or a rhythm, such as:

    FAIL, FAIL, FAIL, SUCCEED

    PROBLEM, PROBLEM, PROBLEM, SOLUTION

    NO, NO, NO, YES

    EXPECTED, EXPECTED, EXPECTED, TWIST

- This is a dramatic tool often used in movies – think: the romantic comedy where the guy's trying to get the girl (fail, fail, fail, succeed). Or a drama where we've been chasing the bad guy, only to find out he's really the goodie (expected, expected, expected, twist). The switch at the end will help you form a clear climax and will normally connect directly to your *idea worth spreading*.

As you approach the summit of your mountain, look to build either a logical or emotional climax. A climax can be formed by:

- **Creating a shift in your talk:** the climax is when your good beats evil, or when your new idea or perspective is fully formed and irrefutable. It's the bit where we overcome challenges and finally succeed.

- **Doing something dramatic:** one of my speakers devised a powerful talk about her struggles with her African identity. She hid for most of the talk, wrapped in a duffel coat. When she flung off her coat to reveal her true African colours, the audience gasped. Magic!

- **Ramping up the passion:** when Martin Luther King Jr's 'I have a dream' speech reached its climax it was because of the power and passion in his voice, as well as his repetition of 'Let freedom ring[!]'. He upped his volume, shortened his sentences and raised his hands to signal that we were reaching the climax of the journey.

- **Returning full circle:** perhaps you set up a question, a challenge or an unsolved problem at the beginning of the talk. Or it could be that you gave a metaphor or story. Now's the moment to return to it.

Examples of build and climax

Benjamin Zander's TED Talk takes us up his mountain of 'we can all appreciate classical music' by showing us step by step how different notes have a different impact on the listener. He balances 'asking' his audience to participate with 'telling' us his expertise. His climax is us appreciating classical music as he plays – masterfully mirroring his message.

When I did my own TEDx Talk, 'Goodbye good girl',[23] I was mindful of these lessons. My build comprises of three key stories about trying and failing to speak my mind. It follows the format FAIL, FAIL, FAIL and then SUCCEED to signal the climax.

Throughout the talk I contrast the 'good' of expressing myself with fierce power (what I called the *bold beast*) versus the 'evil' of wanting to fit in and be liked (what I called the *good girl*). My climax is where the *good girl* faces the *bold beast* and the *bold beast* finally wins. Watch it online and see if you think I manage.

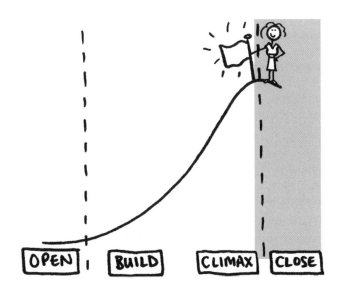

Part 3: The close (approx 10%)

Purpose:

1. Hit home your key message.
2. Call for change.
3. Close the talk with power.

We've reached the summit of our mountain, but the journey doesn't end there – not yet. Just as the rom-com credits don't roll the moment the couple finally get together, in a talk we need a moment to *reach the treasure* of our story and bring it home. That means summarising your key learning points and asking your audience to do something differently as a result of your talk. If you've hit a good climax, your audience are most open to influence at this moment, so don't shy away from speaking with power here. This is where you close the sale, firm up your position as a leading expert, or create the change you seek.

That said, shorter closing sections are often more powerful. Having the energy of the audience raised, we don't want to lose their attention by going on for too long.

Consider again the story of Hillary climbing Everest. We're interested in all the trials and difficulties he faces on the way up, but as soon as he reaches the summit, we've reached our peak of attention. Of course, we know he has to get all the way back down again – and that it probably takes just as long to get down as it did to get up – but we'd rather rejoin Hillary some time later next to the fire with a cognac to hear a few words about what he learned.

What if . . . I don't have much time to prepare?

Expert tip: Paul McGee

'If you don't have time to prepare as thoroughly as this you can still give an impressive performance,' says Paul McGee,[24] one of the UK's leading business speakers. 'The key is to find a story to tell that relates to your key message.

'You'd be surprised how many stories you have or have heard that illustrate your point in a colourful way. Say you're suddenly asked to talk about fireworks. You could ramble on about China, gunpowder, etc. Or you could tell a story about your first bonfire night and what happened to you that made it special.'

Hero's journey and memory

More and more speakers are stepping on stage with limited notes, or none at all. To remember a whole speech is easier than you think if you do the following:

- Keep your journey simple and logical, so you know how one step follows another.
- Rehearse the meaning and thread of the journey, rather than specific words.
- Find key moments to talk around, such as stories.
- Focus on information and stories that you know intimately. As body education expert Moshé Feldenkrais said,[25] 'You can only forget things that you've remembered.'
- If you haven't remembered anything because your structure is logical and balanced, you can't forget anything. This is how some public figures step up on stage with no notes and still manage to say something sensible.

And, since you have created a structure that's neat and memorable for your audience, it will be equally neat and memorable for you.

What if . . . I'm a particularly forgetful person?

Expert tip: David Thomas

'The worst thing you can do to remember a speech is to sit down and try to memorise a pile of cue cards,' says World Memory record holder David Thomas.[26]

'As a memory champion, I can't get away with using notes when I speak in public. So I use the "journey technique" to accurately map out everything I say. It works like this:

1 Create a journey around a building you're familiar with, like your home. You're going to place a different stimulus at different points in your house to help you remember your lines.

2 Start with the front door. If your first message is about sales, imagine a big, white boat sail flapping in the wind at your door.

3 Next, you want to speak about performance, so you step into the front hall and there's Usain Bolt warming up in Lycra shorts, or a Ferrari, or whatever signals performance to you.

4 Keep going through all of the rooms of your house, adding the next part of your speech. The trick is to make each image ridiculous or fun. The more silly the image, the more you have an emotional response and the more you remember.

'Using this method, you can memorise 20 key words in just 12 minutes, which will give you 10 to 20 minutes of speech with no notes. If you forget what you're supposed to be saying, just go back into your house and find the next image.'

Back to balance

Once you've designed your hero's journey, it's time to check the balance of your talk. Given the amount of time you have to speak, are you getting the balance right between the following?

Giving your audience information	vs	Leaving them space to absorb it
Hard-nosed and credible facts	vs	Emotional moments
Moments of fast pace to lift the energy	vs	Moments of reflection
Understanding the audience's current struggles around your subject	vs	Challenging them to do better
Progressing the logic of your argument	vs	Deepening the investigation into each point
Giving frank and bold statements	vs	Evoking the senses

When you reflect on your journey, you may realise it needs a good edit to bring better balance.

Key editing wisdom

Journalist and story coach Beverley Glick gives her 'top 10 editing tips'[27] on what to do if you have too much of the wrong sort of content:

1. **Less is more.** You will need much less content than you think. Allow space for dramatic pauses, audience landing time and off-the-cuff comments.

2. **Return to the idea you want to share.** Remove anything that doesn't support that message.

3. **Think in headlines rather than paragraphs.** Focus on distilling the essence of what you want to say – that way you cut the waffle and it's easier for the audience to remember afterwards.

4. **Speak it out.** Record your talk, listen to it and you'll immediately sense where the narrative doesn't flow or the energy dips. Look for the bits where you stop listening to yourself and cut them.

5. **Draw out key words or themes.** Repeat them at key points during your talk. This will simplify your content and provide anchor points for your audience.

6. **But weed out unnecessary repetition or fillers.** Ask yourself, where would one sentence or idea have more impact than two? If you've made the point with power, then move on.

7. **A simple story will create more resonance than a complex one.** Cut down on the details of what happened and go deeper into details that stimulate the senses, or emotions. These are the bits that are more evocative.

   Complex story: 'It was the week before last and I'd just missed the number 45 bus, so I had to get on the 59, which goes a slightly longer route. And it was raining too and the bus was totally full, so I was feeling really grumpy.'

   Simple story: 'I was squashed under a man's armpit on the number 59 bus. Scowling.'

8. **Kill the clichés, e.g. 'an incredibly life-changing experience', and waste words.** 'In my opinion this is a really interesting idea' can be made more assertive: 'This idea is interesting.'

9. **Use compelling metaphors to show rather than tell.** For example, 'I disappeared into a black hole inside my head' rather than 'I became a bit depressed'.

10. **Drop your best ideas if they don't serve your narrative.** We call this *killing your darlings*. Don't worry though, your darlings can always be resurrected for another talk.

Part

They may forget what you said, but they
will never forget how you made them feel.

Carl W. Buechner

Suzie Talkalot peered down at her long list of bullet points, then up at her audience. Even Ben – best mate, enthusiastic Ben – was slumped down in his seat, checking his phone. Suzie didn't mind public speaking when she was first asked, but she soon realised that people just don't like to listen.

She sighed. 'Why do I always have to be the one who presents the boring information?' she asked herself.

Freshness

In Part 4:

- A new mindset that will make your talks highly memorable.

- Eight powerful ways to use words to bring your talk to life.

- More memorable alternatives to death by PowerPoint.

- How to use interactivity to keep people listening.

If it were possible to commit a public speaking crime, it would be subjecting your audience to a dull, passionless speech. How often have you heard speakers begin with an apology: 'Sorry, I won't take very long' or 'Sorry, it isn't very interesting'?

How many times have you sat in an audience, framing a handout with elaborate doodles while a speaker drones on and on? How many times have you endured a presentation with the same old PowerPoint format? You know the one . . . it has a company logo, a title, four or five neat bullet points and, if you're lucky, a clipart picture in one corner 'to add some fun'.

Aside from being life-sapping for your audience, public speaking that lacks freshness lacks memorability. Neuroscience shows that we remember information more effectively when our mind and senses are engaged. Yet still thousands of audiences every day sit passively listening as a speaker talks.

This will not happen to your audience if you develop the quality of freshness. Part 4 outlines the tools you can use to give your presentations that fizz of freshness which will make every audience sit up, pay attention and – most importantly – remember what you've said.

What is perfect freshness?

- Helping your audience to remember your key message.
- Surprising your audience with innovative, authentic and inspiring moments.
- Creating a public speaking experience for the audience, rather than just another talk to listen to. A public speaking experience means that the audience are engaged in what you're saying; they're *experiencing* it, rather than passively watching your talk (and worse, wishing it were over).
- Being comfortable to change the normal routine. It could be adding more energy and excitement, or it could be adding moments of silence and intensity.
- Selecting the right visual, verbal and interactive tools to make your impact.

The science bit

The hippocampus is the part of the brain that is associated with remembering facts and events. Those facts are later transferred to our cortex, the part of the brain responsible for creating rules and long-term memory. The aim of public speaking, then, is to get your information into your audience's hippocampi. To achieve this, your information needs to be both relevant to your audience (through the quality of empathy) and unique in some way (through freshness).

Remembering the journey

Once you have created your hero's journey from the previous chapter, freshness is the quality that will help you to emphasise the key moments in your talk so that people talk about it afterwards. If the hero's journey is the thread that runs through your talk, freshness adds sparkling beads to the thread.

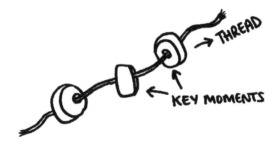

There are so many ways to add a spark of freshness to your talk. But to give you a structure, I'll divide our investigation into what the audience *see*, what they *hear* and what they *do* during your talk.

Get fresh

But before we start on the specifics, to flex your freshness you need to step into a new mindset. This is a mindset in which you are not a public speaker who's delivering a talk, but a public *engager* who's delivering an *experience* to your audience. To do this you'll need bravery and creativity. Here's how you get there.

1. Start by resetting your attitude

When we are children we think anything is possible: 'I want to be an astronaut', 'I'm going to live in a palace' and so on. As we grow up, we acquire rules about what's really possible and how we should behave. Eventually, we get into the world of work and we're encouraged to 'leave our personalities at reception desk, please'.

In this context, it's little wonder that so many people are afraid to step outside the norm of public speaking. As so much of life is based on playing a social role, or hiding or moderating the authentic you, your sense of freshness may feel very rusty indeed. For some, it may seem difficult to so much as smile as they speak, let alone add freshness.

To get fresh, you're going to need a fresh attitude and allow those hidden, childlike thoughts to get through. Freshen up your constraining thoughts:

Unfresh thought	Transformed to
'I *have* to do this'	'I *want* to do this'
'They won't be interested'	'I'm going to make sure they find this interesting'
'I better just get through this'	'I'm going to be playful and enjoy this speaking opportunity'
'Everyone else does their public speaking like this [using PowerPoint, a certain format or a certain style], so I should too'	'If I do the same as everyone else, nobody will remember my talk. This is my chance to try something new and learn from it'
'My audience will probably be bored, but that will have to be OK'	'My audience will be engaged and challenged and that's great!'

If you plan a talk with the second list of thoughts in your head, it will automatically become fresher.

2. Get creative

We understand surprisingly little about how creativity is acquired. Cognitive scientist Paul Thagard makes the best suggestion I've come across, a list of habits highly creative people employ, based on the habits of successful scientists.[28] To get creative he advises:

1. **Make new connections:** don't just use the same old material to create your talk. Look for inspiration from a different field of knowledge and use analogies to link things together.

2. **Don't be afraid of failure:** if you are afraid of doing something wrong, you will restrict your ability to try. Failure is just a sign that you're trying something new and pushing your boundaries, so make it your aim to fail!

3. **Be persistent:** give your new, fresh style a chance to succeed, even if it feels uncomfortable or hits some problems at the start.

4. **Get excited:** nothing is fresher than enthusiasm, so try looking at your topic through the eyes of an excited puppy. What do you like about your topic? Why is it important? What thrilling insight will your talk reveal?

5. **Be sociable:** creative ideas come best when you have new influences, so look to others for ideas about how you can do something different. You could try speaking with a partner to see how that freshens up your performance.

6. **Use the world:** there is inspiration all around you, every moment of your life, if you're just open to it. Seek ideas, metaphors, stories and humour from the world at large. Bring the richness of your experience into your public speaking.

Creativity is a journey, not a destination. Expect your content and delivery to build and evolve over time.

3. Get going!

Building freshness requires a leap outside your comfort zone. There's more on how to manage that in Part 5 on fearlessness. Keep in mind that through freshness you can get to the hearts of your audience. And by getting to their hearts, you can leave them with a powerful, memorable message.

This section gives you a wealth of different ideas for upping the freshness of your performance. But, as with any part of this book, it's up to you to pick the techniques that are most powerful and authentic for you to add to your ingredients list.

Chapter

9

Key wisdom from this chapter

- **Paint pictures with your words:** the words that are most visual are most evocative for an audience. Carefully choose words that bring your talk to life.

- **Great intentional emphasis:** repetition and key words can help your audience to understand and remember your message.

- **Unusual visuals aid memory:** be more memorable by using unusual visual aids, for example a prop.

- **If you must use PowerPoint, make it good:** it's difficult for an audience to remember information that's in the same old format, so bring your presentation to life by using bold or provocative images.

Wonderful words and vibrant visuals

There are endless ways to add that memorable spark of freshness to your public speaking. In this chapter, we'll investigate the different visual and verbal tools at your disposal. Think creatively about how to use each to add texture to your talk.

What they hear: wonderful words

No speaker can get away with avoiding words, so choose your words wisely. They could mean the difference between an 'OK' and a mind-blowing public speaking experience. Let's start with eight devices that help to deliver content in an interesting and memorable way.

Consider your audience as having two types of information needs: left brain needs, or rational, fact-driven needs, and right

brain needs, or emotion-driven needs. This is more or less how the brain works according to neuroscientists, although it's a myth that people are either 'left brainers' or 'right brainers' as much pop psychology suggests – we all use both sides of our brain. Still, different verbal tools are useful to tickle different sides of the brain. Usually a powerful speaker will appeal to both sides. Choose the most appropriate combination of these tools for your message.

1. Powerful quote

For example:

As Einstein said, 'Imagination is more important than knowledge.' In this talk, I'm going to challenge you. You won't just be listening and taking notes, but you'll be cranking up that rusty imagination.

Used for: conjuring inspiration (for the right brain) and adding legitimacy to your point because someone important agrees with you – *if Einstein said it, it must be true* (for the left brain).

Powerful quotes work well at the beginning and end of speeches and are a safe verbal tool to use if you're a nervous speaker. Often quotes are a low-risk method for bringing humour into a speech – quotes from Mark Twain and Oscar Wilde are a good starting point. Create a collection of quotes that fits with your message. Even if you don't use them in the talk, they might be useful if you have a question and answer session afterwards.

2. Stories and famous examples

For example:

Sometimes something happens in life that puts everything else in perspective. When 27-year-old Aron Ralston set off into the wilderness in Utah, he had no idea that he'd arrive home six days later, having escaped from underneath a boulder by amputating his own arm.

Used for: inspiration – *wow, he did that* (for the right brain) and providing evidence – *if Ralston could do something so brave, it must be logically possible* (for the left brain).

Stories and famous examples are ways of adding legitimacy to your argument, while also giving a clear experience for the audience to remember afterwards. If you are telling the whole story though, make sure it is information new to the audience. Aron Ralston's story was made into the film *127 Hours*, so check first who in the audience already knows the story.

What's my story?

Whether you want to touch a single audience as a one-off, or many audiences as a professional speaker, finding 'your story' will help you connect to your audience in a memorable and authentic fashion. Your story is the reason you're qualified to comment on a subject and usually involves an experience that you've gone through that changed your perspective.

You can find your story in even the most mundane of situations: 'On my way to work last week I noticed a young blackbird dancing about in the trees above me. That evening I came home and found it on the ground – a lifeless pile of feathers. That one moment got me thinking of how precious life is.'

Inspirational speakers use their story to add authenticity to their message. If you can deliver your story in a way that's vulnerable and emotional, your performance will carry more power.

3. Analogy/metaphor

For example:

When one crab tries to climb out of a bucket filled with crabs, the others pull him back in. In order to grow, we need to support others in their attempts to change.

Used for: bringing the topic alive (right brain).

A metaphor is a way of understanding one concept by relating it to another. Analogies are extended metaphors. Both can be used extensively in public speaking to create insightful ways of expressing yourself, to get the audience's brains ticking and to help them remember your point. Next time this audience sees a crab in the supermarket, they'll remember the bucket of crabs metaphor and its message.

Metaphors help you to deepen a topic rather than simply tell-ing an audience a message. The brilliant thing about a metaphor is that the audience can build on it. For example, an audience member might contribute, 'Yes, I feel like that crab – and the bucket is all these regulations the government keeps putting on us. I wish they'd just tip us back out into the sea.'

4. Powerful three

For example:

I came. [1] I saw. [2] I conquered. [3]

Or:

There are three things I want you to take from this evening: information [1], inspiration [2] and perspiration [3].

Used for: creating emphasis and emotion (right brain).

Powerful threes create a steady rhythm in speaking that make you sound like a pro. They can be used in conjunction with silence to signal your key messages, or they can be used in the general body of your content to create a rhythm that feels good to the audience.

Threes are deeply embedded in our culture as easy ways to remember things. Most people share the feeling that if they can remember one piece of information, they can probably remem-ber the bit before and the bit after as well – making three things.

There is something intuitively satisfying and effortless about a three. It could be something to do with religion: Christianity has the Holy Trinity and the three Kings; Judaism has the three patriarchs; Hinduism has Brahma the Creator, Vishnu the Pre-server and Shiva the Destroyer; and Buddhism has the Three Jewels, Buddha, Dharma, Sangha.

Since you want to make what you say as effortless as possible for your audience to experience, threes look like a good way to go.

5. Strong fact

For example:

Of the 60,000 thoughts we have every day, 95% of them are the same as yesterday. And 95% of them are the same as tomorrow.

Used for: building evidence (left brain).

Pepper your speech with facts, especially if you have an audience teeming with pragmatists. A strong fact is in some way dramatic and is easy to deliver. Avoid complicated facts such as '35% of people in our sample of women thought they were more than likely to act differently next time if given support by one or more trained specialists' as your audience will be left confused.

Strong facts hit a message more effectively than a pithy statement. Compare the statement 'We all know things are getting more expensive' with a fact like 'In the past ten years, consumer goods increased in price by 30%'. Facts add to your credibility as a speaker. Remember to research your facts well, so that if someone questions you, you're able to give them your source.

A brilliant example of the power of facts is Laura Bates' talk on 'Everyday sexism' from TEDxCoventGardenWomen. She lists fact after fact that demonstrate how men and women still aren't equal. The strength of her use of facts comes first from her choice of facts – they cover so many different angles that they're impossible to refute – and second, she knows the facts, so they're not abstract – they feel meaningful to her and therefore to the audience.

6. Evocative image

One of my trainers, journalist Beverley Glick, elicited a whole emotional journey through words alone:

Those days I lived the champagne lifestyle of a rock journalist. On a rare holiday in an Indian village I was already bored. My chauffeur suggested he take me to his humble apartment and I apathetically agreed. As we pulled up outside his crumbling home, I sneered slightly and tried to ignore the stench of putrid rubbish. His wife greeted me at the door. Her eyes sparkling with joy, she welcomed me in. I tentatively sat down and noticed with disgust that she was pouring me warm, flat Coca-Cola. I almost got up to leave. And then she turned to me and bowed, offering me the cup of warm, flat Cola in both hands like the most precious of gifts. My champagne lifestyle suddenly felt like the emptiest place in the world.[29]

Used for: getting the audience to visualise and connect with you. Adding emotion and drama (right brain).

To create an evocative image, think like a novelist. A good author might not write, 'Dave was a really nasty man', but she might write, 'Dave slammed the door as he left, scowled at his elderly neighbour and kicked her cat out of his way'. By adding colour and detail to your performance you give the audience a visual image, something to latch on to. Your talk becomes instantly more memorable as a result. Don't forget the other senses, too – evoke the sound of snow crunching under your feet, the smell of bread coming out of the oven, the texture of a kitten's fur, or the taste of a sour lemon, twisting your mouth.

7. Humour/telling jokes

Sir Ken Robinson started his much viewed 2006 TED Talk[30] by saying:

Good morning. How are you? It's been great, hasn't it? I've been blown away by the whole thing. In fact, I'm leaving.

Used for: entertaining and building rapport (right brain).

Humour like this example has the capacity to open up an audience and connect them to your message. Yet often we can use humour in the wrong way. Before you use humour, ask yourself: how relevant is your humour to what you're trying to achieve? Is your joke a triumphant trumpet signalling that what's coming is an entertaining, witty speech like Ken Robinson's TED Talk? Is it a funny insight that frames your perspective on the topic? Both of these would be excellent uses of humour.

Or is it an attempt to get your audience to listen for 20 seconds before the real, boring part of your speech starts? They say, 'once you've made an audience laugh, you've won them over', but this is only assuming you continue to engage your audience rather than bore them.

Another important element to humour is to develop your own style. We imagine that the audience will only like us if we're funny, and we desperately want to be liked, so shouldn't we tell a joke? Not necessarily. If the traditional idea of funny doesn't work for you, find your own way to make the audience laugh.

What if . . . I'm not funny?

Expert tip: John Hotowka

Professional speaker John Hotowka mixes his own brand of humour with magic to create an entertaining experience for his audiences: 'If you're worried about being funny, you're on the wrong track,' he says.[31] 'Trying to be funny doesn't work, because the audience can tell a mile off if you're not being authentic. Focus on being entertaining instead as the purpose of your talk is much more important than getting your audience to laugh. A drama on TV isn't necessarily funny, but it can still be entertaining.

'If you want to use humour, "go ugly early" by testing your material out on a smaller audience. A lot of comedians do this before their tour, to see how well their material works in a low-risk environment.

'If you're used to raising a laugh, but your audience don't seem to be responding, don't worry. Just let it go, be authentic and polite and keep talking.'

8. Repetition, repetition, repetition

For example:

In his much viewed TEDx Talk, marketing guru Simon Sinek[32] repeated five times: 'People don't buy what you do, they buy why you do it.'

Used for: adding credibility to your concepts (left brain). Building resonance or inspiration (right brain).

Repeated phrases or words give your key message time to come to the boil and ensure that we remember it. They are a useful rhythm to develop along your hero's journey – a signpost of sorts that reminds us what the key message is. Repetition brings much needed emphasis.

Even if we think what we're saying is clear and obvious, remember that you've heard your argument many times before. The audience are not hanging on every word and need your signal about which words are worth remembering or writing down. But be careful not to sound repetitive in your repetition. Simon Sinek deepened his argument every time he repeated this phrase by giving a different anecdote and revealing a new insight, which always connected to the phrase 'people don't buy what you do, they buy why you do it'. As a result his argument was strengthened each time.

Vibrant visuals

Words alone can be very powerful, but visual aids add something extra for the memory to latch on to. Let's turn to the different visuals at your disposal and how you might use them in the freshest way possible.

Start with innovation

Let's imagine that the projector's broken and you can't use PowerPoint. Don't panic, it's not the end of the world. One of the best ways to engage your audience is to use a prop.

Because 3D objects aren't commonly used in speaking, they often provide an unforgettable connection to your message.

One of my speakers, Yang-May Ooi, a lawyer, fully embraced the concept of freshness as she was developing a talk about the Chinese tradition of foot binding. She used a prop in her talk that I'll remember for ever. She carefully evoked in our minds the image of the tiny foot of a Chinese girl in the 18th century, placed that foot gently on the ground and – wham – hit that spot on the floor hard with a chair. It represented the painful process of foot binding, where the child's foot was broken again and again to keep it small and 'ladylike'.

You can tell when a moment in a talk is fresh – because that's the bit that people talk about afterwards. The force of that moment in Yang-May's speech is a talking point to this day. In fact, Yang-May embraced freshness so much that her short talk on foot binding has become a one-woman West End play (*Bound Feet Blues*).

Your prop may be less (or more!) extreme, but take care that:

- the prop is big enough for everyone to see
- you don't have too many props causing clutter – less is more
- your prop is relevant to the topic. Does everyone see the connection between the prop and the topic, or do you need to explain it?

Think of symbols and metaphors relating to your message that could become props. An accountant reminding an audience of tax return deadlines might hold up a giant brown envelope; a nutritionist speaking about diet and brittle bones might bring breadsticks to snap; and a speaker emphasising the many hats they wear might bring a selection of hats to change into at different points of the talk.

PowerPoint

If you must use a projected image, aspire to make it the most exciting visual your audience have ever seen. The risk of PowerPoint visuals is that they send us into a viewer mentality, as though we're sitting at the cinema eating popcorn. Except there's no popcorn and the movie we're watching is utterly, utterly dull. You've probably seen that 'movie' before:

- title on the top of the page
- four neat bullet points down the side
- company logo in one corner
- and (if the speaker's feeling really exotic) a clipart in the other corner.

The problem with this, other than it being exceptionally dull, is that the audience's brains will react as if they've already seen your ideas before and they will be much less likely to recall your message later.

Do your audience really need another presentation?

Although many speakers feel naked without a PowerPoint, you can seem more competent and refreshing as a speaker if you don't use it. I tend to avoid PowerPoint, especially when I'm running a small group workshop, as it discourages participation.

Using PowerPoint is a personal choice you should make based on your empathetic understanding of your audience's needs. If you're speaking to a large audience or have a technical or precise message, using PowerPoint might be the right choice. But there's still no excuse for making it dull.

TED Talk favourite, statistician Hans Rosling,[33] is an excellent example of a speaker who brings his visuals alive. In one talk he charts population statistics as they move over time, speaking about them like a commentator at a horse race: 'And China is gaining . . . yes! It's taking over Russia.'

If you do use PowerPoint, challenge yourself to do the following:

- Emphasise only the key facts on screen.
- Use a minimum of words and a maximum of images.
- Make your images compelling and even provocative.
- Blank out the PowerPoint by pressing the 'black' key on your clicker, or the full stop on your laptop. You'll be amazed at the effect on the audience – it's like watching Sleeping Beauty awake from her slumber.
- Use your full expression and stage presence so that *you* are the main focus of the talk and your PowerPoint is exactly what it should be – a visual aid rather the talk itself.

Flipchart

A much neglected public speaking tool, the flipchart is a great, versatile visual aid that works well for groups of up to 40 people (sometimes more). I often use a flipchart to draw cartoons and diagrams for my audiences and find it much more human and authentic than PowerPoint. Even if you can't draw, think of all the fresh uses a blank sheet of paper might have for your audience: it could be a treasure map of instructions, an entertaining diagram, a quote, a game of Hangman and so on. And because you are building it together, it becomes a useful and memorable visual prompt.

With a bit of time spent thinking about your audience's needs and the unique parts of your message, you can create some innovative ways to use your flipchart. As you do that, make sure you avoid these three flipchart foes:

1. 'I'm sorry, does that say "Mother" or "Monster"?'

If your writing looks like a spider's run across the page, or you can't spell 'toffee', let alone spell *for* toffee, then think twice before using a flipchart. As an alternative, either pre-prepare your flipchart, or invite a neat writer from the audience to take notes. Stick to block capitals so that your audience can clearly see your writing from a distance.

2. 'Whoops, the pen's run out'

There's nothing that kills the freshness of a quick brainstorm like checking one, two, three, four pens to find one that still has ink in it. If you use a flipchart regularly, bring your own marker pens with you and test them before you start.

3. 'Nice bum, shame about the face'

It's often useful to have one speaker talking to the audience and another taking notes on a flipchart. However, you may need to manage a group discussion and write at the same time. If this happens, avoid blocking the writing by standing directly in front of your flipchart, bum sticking out at the audience. Try writing from the side so that everyone can see what you're writing as you go.

Top tip

Hidden handwriting

If you write some notes in light pencil on a flipchart, your audience won't be able to see them. While you're brainstorming, you can keep track of your key questions and topic areas without ever needing to look at your notes.

Handouts

In formal talks and meetings, handouts can be an effective way to complement the structure of your talk, or to go alongside your other visual aids. Use handouts when you're giving detailed information, when the audience may need to analyse or reflect on what you're saying, or when they need to write something down. Here's how to make handouts work for you:

- **Take one, pass it on:** avoid sending handouts round the audience during your talk. There will be too much paper rustling, you waste precious speaking time and people will look at the new, exciting handout rather than at you. For handouts that summarise your talk, allow people to collect a copy after you've finished speaking. For handouts that you're using during the session, make sure they're ready and waiting for the audience when they enter the room. Request that the audience resist the urge to flick forwards in the handouts.

- **'Print six slides to a page':** avoid the temptation to give your audience printed copies of your dull PowerPoint slides after your talk. While audiences think they like the comfort of receiving the slides from a great talk, they're not as useful as we all think. How many times have you actually looked at slides after you've listened to a speech? Not very often, I suspect. Slides for a talk tend to be irrelevant without you speaking around them, unless your slides are laden with too much information. You're much better off spending a few minutes crafting your slides into an appealing briefing pack that your audience will keep and refer to later.

- **Fill in the gap:** to help emphasise your key message, encourage audience members to add their own notes and insights to your diagrams, bullet points or pictures as you talk. Leave gaps that they can fill in – and signal to them 'this goes in box four, write it down now'. Your audience should feel they've got something from hearing you talk that they couldn't have read in an article written by you.

- **Stay in touch:** be sure to include your contact details so your audience can get in touch if they want – it's a great way to build your credibility as an expert.

Going fresh

Those are some ideas from me, so what else can you do creatively with your visuals? Here are a few ideas my clients and I have used in the past:

- Smash something! In my TEDx Talk 'Goodbye good girl' I got a cup made from sugar glass and smashed it on stage to make a point.
- Use different colours for different types of message. Everything about the past could be red, everything about the present orange and everything about the future green.
- Fill the wall with colourful quotes relating to your subject. I print out humorous public speaking quotes and place them around my workshop rooms for added inspiration during breaks.
- Use your audience as a visual aid. I've worked with kids in the past, so I sometimes get very childish with my audience. If the atmosphere is right I invite adult audience members up on stage to become my key message. I've had audience members wearing the *Crown of Freshness*, the *Belt of Fearlessness* and the *Bra of Authenticity* to emphasise the three qualities I want them to take away. These were all made from scraps of paper a few hours before. Ridiculous, but people remember those talks more than anything else I do.
- One of my speakers, Sarah Hyndman, is a font expert. She recreates stories like *Star Wars* using different fonts alone: a sciency font for R2-D2, a sinister font for Darth Vader and so on – something that's totally innovative and memorable.

The sky's the limit with fresh visuals. Have fun, be bold and you'll create a little magic.

> **What if . . . my audience won't accept innovation?**
>
> *Expert tip: David Hyner*
>
> 'There's no such thing as an audience who dislike innovation,' says professional speaker David Hyner,[34] 'but sometimes speakers worry about this because they lack imagination or confidence. So many

speakers stick to familiar territory and end up delivering the same boring presentation as everyone else, but it doesn't have to be that way.

'I once worked with the CEO of a large company who knew he had some difficult figures to present at his company conference. He could have given the long, serious presentation that everyone expected, but instead he came on stage to pyrotechnics and the 'Mission Impossible' theme tune, abseiling through the ceiling! That presentation is still talked about to this day.

'If you're confident, your audience will accept whatever innovative techniques or explanations you throw at them. If you prefer a less dramatic way of innovating, look to respected professionals in your field for inspiration. I often interview top performers to gain inspiration from them about how to present my subject. Their enthusiasm and quality of thinking gives me fresh ideas and at the very least I have an interesting story to share about interviewing them.'

Key wisdom from this chapter

- **Interactivity aids learning:** if we listen we are more likely to switch off, but if we participate in a talk we'll remember it more and enjoy it more.

- **Rhetorical questions are good, aren't they?** Devices that get your audience to reflect on what you're saying help them to feel involved in your talk.

- **Interactivity brings delicious uncertainty:** try asking the audience to raise their hands, complete a task or answer a question to give them a say in the talk. Then tailor it to their needs.

- **Try facilitating a conversation with the audience:** whether it's a large or small audience, a group discussion brings energy to the room.

- **The best learning happens through experience:** if you really want the audience to learn, get them to do something practical. While this may require more lateral thinking with a big audience, practical experiences are the most memorable of all.

Ingenious interactivity

Listening is tiring for audiences. Researchers believe that most adults can focus on one thing for a maximum of 20 minutes, after which they need to re-focus to stay interested. That means that if you leave the audience just watching you talk for a long period of time without re-engaging them, you increase the chance they'll drift off.

Interaction, however, is energising. As experiential learning theorists have demonstrated, interactivity can engage an audience in your subject matter, meaning that they're more likely to remember your message after you've finished speaking.

Depending on your audience size, their needs and your confidence, there are four levels of interactivity you might use with them. See which of these you can use to bring freshness into your speaking.

Interactivity level 1: rhetorical interaction

The first level of interaction is the lowest risk: involving the whole audience, without them needing to do anything physically. Rhetorical interaction is moving the audience's attention from 'What's the speaker saying?' to 'How does what the speaker's saying apply to me?' You are getting the grey cells working, meaning that you will begin to have a room of learners rather than simply listeners. Ken Robinson uses rhetorical interaction masterfully in his popular TED Talk,[35] making the audience feel as though they are having a conversation – 'Am I wrong?' he asks.

Different methods of rhetorical interaction

(a) Rhetorical questions: e.g. 'How would you feel if you put yourself in my position?' or 'How does this affect your business?' or 'What would you do if you had to make a choice between the right thing and the thing that's expected of you?'

(b) Applying a fact to the audience: e.g. 'More than one in three people will develop some form of cancer during their life. That's a tough statistic, but until it affects your life, cancer is a distant difficulty. Take a look at the neighbour either side of you and ask yourself, "Which one of us will it be?" Now how distant does cancer feel?'

(c) Stimulating memory recall: e.g. 'Many of us have fond memories of close, personal time with Sophie during her life' [signals audience to recall a personal time spent with Sophie] or 'We all remember our first day at school' [signals the audience to recall their first day at school].

What level 1 interaction is good for

Rhetorical interaction is great when you don't have the time, physical space or resources available to do a more in-depth interactive exercise. Some key moments when you might use rhetorical interaction include:

- a 60-second introduction to yourself or your topic
- a speech format where it's not expected for you to interact with the audience – perhaps the audience is too big, perhaps the occasion is too formal, or perhaps you are being videoed with no microphones for the audience
- during impromptu speaking – rather than following your instinct to only talk about yourself, turn your topic onto your audience. Even if this is unrehearsed, it will show you to be a skilled speaker. Start with phrases like 'What if you . . . ?', 'Imagine you were . . . ' or 'Ever thought of . . . ?'

Interactivity level 2: individual task

An individual task is something you ask your audience members to do to concrete your message. Typically these are 'in the seats' exercises and can start as briefly as a 'hands up if you . . . ' question, much like Jamie Oliver uses in his TED Talk[36] when he asks the audience how many of them have children, nephews or nieces. Here you are shifting the audience dynamic from a one-way information flow – 'I'll just listen and gather information' – to a two-way interaction – 'I'm also involved in this talk'. This creates a delicious uncertainty, where the audience knows that this talk is being tailored to their needs, rather than just being wheeled out for the hundredth time. Practical interaction increases memory recall and places the responsibility on the audience to learn.

Types of individual tasks

Note taking

A simple form of individual interaction is encouraging your audience to take notes, or to write down your contact details. It's not the most innovative technique, but it's often neglected. Good note taking has been shown not only to be a source of information for audience members to refer back to but also to be a process to help memory recall. Encourage note taking by:

- asking your audience to take notes: 'There'll be a lot of information in this talk, so please feel free to take notes. I'll give you a moment now to get your notebooks out'
- reiterating key points: 'And this is a point you'll want to note down'
- allowing the audience time to jot down key facts.

Quiz

Personalise your message by either getting your audience to test their knowledge on a subject (e.g. a right/wrong answer quiz) or testing their attitude towards it (e.g. a personality questionnaire). Quizzes often add a lively and competitive feeling to a room. After you've finished the quiz, bring the learning from it back to the whole room by getting audience members to share their answers. You can do this by a show of hands or by asking individuals for their answer.

If you're feeling bold, jazz up a quiz into a lively game by getting audience members to 'vote with their feet' and move to the part of the room that represents their answer – 'If you agree, head to the left of the room, if you disagree, head to the right of the room.'

Individual exercise

Go deeper with your audience by getting them to put your information into practice. You could ask your audience to write down their answers to a series of questions, complete a diagram, draw something, or any number of other possibilities. Exercises are important where you have a strong learning message and would like to test the audience's ideas or abilities while you're in the same room. Exercises are often, but not necessarily, supported by handouts.

Think creatively to see how you can avoid the cliché exercise and also meet the audience's needs.

Question and answers

This is the most common interaction in large audiences. It is your choice as to whether to accept questions throughout your talk, or whether you'd like to focus on them at the end. For many speakers, the idea of a Q&A is the most nerve-wracking part of a speech or presentation. Don't worry, you're not expected to know all the answers.

Note that question and answers sessions often only involve those who are asking the question and as such can be boring for those who have already decided they don't want to ask a question. To engage more of your audience in a Q&A, you could ask 'hands up' questions, e.g. 'How many of you have had a near-death experience?', 'How many of you know someone who has?', 'How many of you would consider yourselves religious?'

Stand up, sit down

A favourite innovative individual task of mine uses individuals in the audience as a visual aid. Choose statistics that are key to your message and use your audience to be those statistics: 'Imagine that all of us in this room represent the global population. Can I ask this half of the room [gesture to 50% of the audience] to stand up please. All of those standing together own just 1% of the world's wealth. Now I'd like this group to stand up [gesture to about 30% of the audience] – you own about 6% of the world's wealth.

'Now may I ask the rest of you to stand up, apart from you [gesture to a small cluster of people representing 1% of the audience] – you together own about half of the world's wealth.

And now, let's have the final people in the room standing. These [two or three] individuals – just them on their own – own 43% of the world's wealth. How does that make the rest of you feel?'

You could also combine this interaction with visual aids. In this example, you might illustrate each group you refer to with an image on a PowerPoint slide, or you could 'give a gift' to each group, the first group getting a small bread bun to share and the last group getting the keys to the entire bakery.

What level 2 tasks are good for

Individual tasks are usually used where you have a large number of people but your room layout prohibits them from interacting well with each other, such as when the layout is theatre format. Here, the audience don't expect to interact with each other, so communication channels are between the speaker and individual audience members, rather than within the audience. Scenarios where this might be the case include:

- academic lectures where you typically find fixed seating – beware a lecture with no interaction as it makes it easy for the audience to fall asleep
- groups or workshops when there isn't time for audience members to work together
- large audiences of an almost limitless size. Even in an audience of thousands I have seen motivational speakers like Tony Robbins involving the audience – so you can, too.

Good individual interaction engages all of the audience with the task. To make that happen, be assertive and clear with what you're asking them to do. Stick to your requests with confidence and you'll soon have everyone participating.

Interactivity level 3: information sharing

The third level of audience interaction is between members of the audience as well as with you. A century of educational research has shown that collaboration between learners improves the amount of information they recall.

When you engage in information-sharing activities, your role evolves into one of a facilitator, rather than just a public speaker. This is a useful role for you to play because:

- together you have more information than just you alone
- it takes the pressure off you to know all the answers
- most people love to talk! If you give your audience a chance to hear their own voice, they're more likely to leave thinking, 'Wow, that was a really great talk.'

Types of information sharing

Pair share

Some audiences will need warming up to interaction, such as if you're faced with a room of snowmen (see p. 78). The pair share is a great way to encourage sharing in a way that feels low risk to audience members. Simply ask the audience to discuss a question in pairs, then ask volunteers to share what they've learned with the whole room. This method is effective when wrapping up the key messages of your session, e.g. 'Tell your partner the main thing you want to do differently when you've left this room.' Individuals may not want to share such information with the whole room, but sharing with a partner may feel more comfortable.

The snowball

As an extension of the pair share, you can use a snowball to debate an idea through the whole room. This works well if you'd like to develop consensus in an audience containing many diverse opinions:

1. After a pair share, get the pairs to bundle together with another pair and discuss a question, e.g. 'What is the future for our organisation?'. The group of four should come to a consensus.

2. Next, get each group of four to combine with another group of four who have a different opinion and discuss the question again. Once again, consensus should be reached.

3. You can continue doing further rounds for as long as it takes to achieve consensus within the whole audience.

Usually two or three rounds are enough, before discussions begin to get repetitive.

4. Bring the discussion back to the whole room and ask each group to comment about the consensus that was reached.

Facilitated discussion

To facilitate a discussion is to help your audience express thoughts and ideas relating to your topic. Your role is no longer to provide information but to help others to express their ideas; to challenge those ideas and to draw themes from the group that further your key messages. By involving the audience in a form of discussion, they will more effectively remember your message and will be able to apply that information in different settings afterwards.

Some rules of good facilitation:

1. **Agree your role with the audience:** explain that your role will not be to give your opinion but to facilitate the discussion. This is particularly important in discussions that might become personal or emotional. If your authority is agreed with the audience, you will have their support if, for example, you need to stop a thread of discussion that is counterproductive.

2. **Start with the right question:** the question framing your discussion should be well thought through. Test your question with a few friends or colleagues by brainstorming the answers they would give. Does your question lead the discussion in the right direction?

3. **Manage the discussion:**

   - Use clear, powerful questions to encourage audience members to develop a deeper understanding of arguments and ideas. This is useful for all facilitators as they try to open up the audience to new ways of looking at the topic.

   - Curate the conversation: if an audience member is taking up too much air time or bringing little benefit, take firm control to keep the conversation on track. Cut in at a pause and thank them for their input; ask them to be brief with their answers; or set the expectation in advance that everyone should be brief and focused with their input.

   - Involve all members of the audience: spread the discussion to members of the group who aren't participating fully. Encourage those quieter audience members by asking them open questions such as 'What do you think?' rather than closed questions such as 'Do you agree?' Assume that everyone has useful input to give.

4. **Manage yourself:** the way a facilitator behaves will be reflected in how the group behaves. So, if you are anxious or overly curt with facilitation, the level of tension will increase in the group and you may find a heated discussion developing. If you stay calm, so will the general atmosphere within your audience, even if one or two members of the group find the topic emotional.

Group tasks

These involve splitting your audience into sub-groups. In a group task, individuals share information within a group of three to six and answer questions or complete an activity together. Some group tasks include:

- discussing a question together and brainstorming the answers on a flipchart

- group members sharing opinions on the subject at hand
- completing a quiz together, in competition with other groups.

Group challenges are a fantastic way to spread the learning within the room and to help your audience interact more closely with the subject matter. They are particularly effective when you have audience members seated around tables, or with plenty of room to move chairs into small circles.

What level 3 interactions are good for

Information sharing is most relevant when you'd like your audience to interact with your topic and apply their own thinking to it. It's also a useful and productive way to fill time in a speaking schedule, because one exercise could last anything from a couple of minutes to a number of hours. Information sharing works best in a small to medium-sized group, but it can also work well in larger groups if you have enough:

- space to move: for example, a lecture theatre is a more difficult format for information sharing within the audience because of fixed seating
- time for people to discuss: remember that interactive discussions often take longer than you think.

Some conference facilities are now offering live Twitter 'back channelling' screens to help larger audiences interact with their speaker. This is a time-saving and modern way to engage in discussion with your audience and it also allows you to interact with an audience who may not even be in your room, through live streaming. But make sure you can switch off the Twitter stream if it becomes distracting. Cliff Atkinson has written a book, *The Backchannel*,[37] explaining how to duck the dangers of social media's new influence in public speaking.

Information-sharing interactions can be energising and exciting, but they can also be difficult to predict or manage. Don't enter this kind of interaction if you have a short time-frame. For highly factual messages where an expert is imparting information (such as a legal briefing), or highly personal messages where your story doesn't need to be commented on (such as a speech or toast), information-sharing activities are unlikely to be relevant.

Interaction level 4: learning by doing

This final level of audience interaction immerses your audience in a journey where they're learning from a practical situation you go through together.

Types of learning by doing activities

Experiential games and simulations

A step on from a group challenge is to design a game or simulation in which audience members play a role in an activity as if it were real life. If a game sounds too flippant or unprofessional to be worthwhile, keep in mind that research shows games not only increase interest in your topic but also increase the learning a participant retains.

To gain confidence in the effectiveness of game playing, you'd greatly benefit from speaking to young people at least once in your career. Young people are quite happy to show when they're bored, in a way that we learn to hide later in life. Bring out a game and you'll see not only how much they enjoy it but also how powerful this format is for creating fresh and memorable experiences.

I often use games in my workshops to demonstrate a learning point. One of my favourites is the 'UM Game', where participants are challenged to explain words on a card without saying any 'ums' or 'erms'. This builds their awareness and is a lot of fun.

Whenever I have transferred games into an adult learning context, no matter how 'formal' the situation, they have gone down well, so long as I clearly explain the relevance of the game to the topic. Sometimes adults even become more competitive than the kids! Games are at their most effective when participants are debriefed skilfully, through good facilitation.

Other experiential games and simulations I've used include:

- putting together a jigsaw puzzle as a group (great for 'piecing together the big picture' messages)
- building a bridge, straw tower, paper animal or collage (used for all sorts of messages: time management, resource management, team working, etc.)
- drawing with a blindfold while the other person gives instructions (the importance of clear communication).

There's no limit with experiential games. Bear in mind that such exercises can take some time to prepare, but your audience will appreciate the effort you put in.

The laboratory

Some messages are based around practical skills that are best cemented into the minds of your audience by practice and feedback in a safe laboratory. For example, the most powerful and memorable thing I can do for my public speaking students is to encourage them to get up in front of an audience and speak. By going through the motions in a safe environment, they are able to learn lessons that are far deeper than any other form of speaking. If you have a lot of time, a small audience and a skills-focused message to deliver, practice is the most powerful and practical technique I can think of.

You could do the same with a course on writing, leadership, marketing – all manner of topics.

You can make your laboratory most effective by:

- making sure the practice simulation is as close to life as possible, by using real-life examples that relate to the audience

- giving feedback on each person's performance – if you have too many participants to do this yourself, get the audience to give each other feedback
- linking your laboratory practice to the learning content that you've offered the audience earlier in your talk.

What learning by doing interactions are good for

Learning by doing is the most interactive set of tools. These techniques are most frequently seen in learning environments such as workshops and conference breakouts, but with a bit of lateral thinking you could also do a practical activity in a formal speech. To run a good learning by doing exercise, be sure to:

- allow plenty of time and physical space for the interaction
- practise well before you do your exercise for the first time, so that you're aware of what questions will be in the minds of your audience
- expect a few members of the audience to need persuasion to get fully involved in the exercise – have it clear in your mind why you are doing the task and what benefit participants will get from it
- keep a back-up activity in mind if your exercise is new, in case it doesn't work – information-sharing interactions are often good to have as back-up
- end by bringing the whole group back together to summarise the key things you have learned.

Part

5

Courage is resistance to fear,
mastery of fear, not absence of fear.

Mark Twain

Sonia Speakwell took a deep breath as she stepped onto the stage. She'd finally made it to deliver her TED Talk and she wasn't going to let the moment get the better of her.

She centred herself for a moment, letting the room fall silent. Then she lifted her sparkly eyes to meet the audience, smiled and started speaking.

Her heart was thumping in her chest, but Sonia knew that what she had to say was far more important than her nerves. She wanted to take them right there, to Somalia, where it had all begun for her. And she knew it had to come from her heart.

Fearlessness

In Part 5:

- Public speaking is an act of leadership – see how this perspective can make you fearless.

- How to harness your nerves and turn them into excitement that can benefit your audience.

- Methods for accessing your full fearless power as a speaker.

By developing your awareness, empathy, balance and freshness, you can master the art of doing a solid job as a public speaker. But is 'solid' enough? If you want to become a speaker who can influence and inspire, you'll want the extra power brought only by fearlessness.

Consider those rare moments of passion when a speaker stands up and speaks from a place of fearlessness. They are not always popular with those around them. Yet from Jesus to Gandhi, Churchill to Martin Luther King Jr, Emmeline Pankhurst to Malala Yousafzai, these fearless speakers have inspired and provoked change in the world through the power of their words and actions. This is the true power of public speaking.

From *Charlie Hebdo*'s cartoons, to a corporate board member calling their colleagues out on corruption, freedom of speech is more important now than ever. If you can develop the quality of fearlessness, you can also be the one to step up in the crucial moment to say 'No' or 'Let's do this differently'.

Public speaking is an act of *leadership*. Our audiences are looking to us to change something, teach them, or lead them somewhere. We simply must embrace our leadership qualities to be the best speaker we can.

Why aren't we fearless?

Layers of public speaking fear combine with the social threat of being rejected for our beliefs. This is natural – it's the predator reflex I mentioned in Chapter 3. The desire to avoid the gaze of predators causes us to shrink, hide and moderate our personalities. We seek to fit in rather than stand out, which is probably why dull PowerPoint slides are so popular. They are low risk and we can't be attacked for using them because that's what everyone else is doing.

Yet if you truly wish for your public speaking to be powerful, fitting in should be precisely the opposite of your aim. It's a scary thought. And that's why we need fearlessness.

Fearless is not the same as 0% fear

Importantly, fearlessness isn't about somehow destroying your fear, or suppressing it. Even professional speakers feel fear (or nerves, or anxiety, or tension) to some degree before an important public speaking gig. The key difference between nervous beginners and professionals is that the professionals have learned not to take their fear seriously. Fearlessness is about transforming the energy of anticipation from fear to excitement.

As first suggested by the 19th-century scholars William James and Carl Lange, emotions are bodily experiences that we attach a meaning to – like or dislike. When we look at it, we can see that fear and excitement are two sides of the same coin. Imagine waiting in a queue for a rollercoaster with two friends. The first friend hates rollercoasters, the second loves them. As you're queuing, the first friend is imagining all the horrible things that could happen: getting stuck at the top, falling out of the seat, being sick and so on. In the queue, they're feeling a sensation in their body (something like butterflies), they're imagining that something bad will happen and attaching a meaning to that feeling – FEAR.

The second person is imagining all the wonderful things that will happen on that same rollercoaster: the whoosh of speed, the tummy jumping feeling, wind in the hair and so on. They're also feeling the same sensation in their body – something like butterflies. But this time they're imagining that something *good* will happen and attaching a different meaning to that feeling – EXCITEMENT.

In the body, fear and excitement are exactly the same thing: energy. It's our attitude that determines how we use that energy. Fear is anticipating a negative outcome from a situation. Excitement is anticipating a positive outcome. Anticipating something negative causes us to freeze, rush, procrastinate or avoid. Anticipating something positive causes us to dive in without over-analysing.

Fearlessness, then, is about harnessing the energy of your fear and using it to serve your audience.

What is perfect fearlessness?

- Seeing public speaking as an act of leadership that brings change.
- Using the full force of your personality to benefit your audience.
- Sticking up for your beliefs, even if they are unpopular.
- Embracing 'fear' as energy that is needed in your speaking.
- Welcoming mistakes and learning from them.
- Always focusing on what will bring benefit to your audience – even if it goes beyond your comfort zone.

Chapter

11

Key wisdom from this chapter

- **Inspiring speaking means creating positive change:** the greatest speakers combine a strong message with the desire to benefit the audience.

- **Find your fight:** use your sense of inner purpose to bring a powerful core of meaning to your speaking. This might come out as an explicit message, or your speaking might be more subtly influenced. Either way, you will be a more fearless speaker.

- **Do it for your audience:** if you're too nervous to speak for your own sake, do it for the audience you seek to benefit.

- **Visualise yourself into success:** if you can see yourself speaking with power, you're already on your way. Try a visualisation technique to give yourself permission to be a great speaker.

- **Make a promise of how you want to be:** design yourself an image of how you are when you're at your most fearless. This is your speaker's promise. Remind yourself to be this every time you stand up to speak.

Going beyond fear

Inspiring speaking

There are four territories we can claim as public speakers:

Impact of your speaking		2. Bullying	4. Inspiring speaking
	High impact		
	Low impact	1. Lecturing	3. 'Friendly chat'
		Self-serving/Egocentric	Servant speaking/Empathetic
		Intention of your speaking	

1. Lecturing

By lecturing I mean talking *at* the audience, rather than hoping to offer them something of benefit. A physicist friend of mine says that at conferences his academic colleagues seem to battle to see whose research can be presented in the most difficult-to-grasp way. It's as if you are more intelligent if fewer people in the audience can understand your topic. For me this is public speaking cowardice – if nobody understands you, your ideas can't be criticised. It's a defence mechanism. And naturally it means that the audience benefit much less from your ideas.

2. Bullying

Then you have speakers who are really there to serve *their* aims rather than those of the audience. Often there's a strong sales pitch involved. While there's nothing inherently wrong with selling from stage, I've seen many 'motivational speakers' use manipulative techniques to trick audience members into buying hugely expensive products on stage that the buyer can't really afford – and that the speaker in private admits 'aren't particularly good'.

When the bright lights of a stage puff up our egos, we have to stay aware of whether we're really seeking to serve our audience, or whether we're pushing them into something that won't benefit them long term. The extreme example of this type of speaker was Hitler. Sure, he had a powerful impact on his audiences, but his was to bully and manipulate them towards hatred for others. For this reason I could never label Hitler an inspiring speaker, or a fearless one. Hatred, in my opinion, always comes from fear.

3. 'Friendly chat'

As I mentioned in Part 2, if we seek to benefit our audience we're on the right path. But if we lack impact in our speaking it can be little more than a 'friendly chat'. This is the territory of the speaker who wishes to be liked more than they wish to tell the truth. Many of our more likeable politicians fall into this category, for instance Boris Johnson, who always seems to pre-empt the audience's criticisms of him and align with them, using humour and quirky language to add to his appeal. Great empathy, but it can be unclear what he really stands for. And if it's not clear what a speaker stands for, I don't know how to act as a result of their words.

4. Inspiring speaking

Inspiring speaking, then, is the territory where we go fearlessly beyond our own ego needs and beyond the need to be loved. Here we create change. Far from being a place that's reserved for the 'greats', we can step into inspiring speaking whenever we like – by letting the power of our message surpass our doubts and fears.

When this happens, technique and rules become less important. *You* become less important. Instead, you become a symbol for the change that you seek in the world. Your message is *through you*, but not *about you*, even if the talk includes a personal story. What is of utmost importance is the *change that is brought about for the audience* – everything else is secondary.

The consequences of stepping into inspiring speaking are vast:

- Nerves are naturally channelled into useful energy.
- You feel in flow with your audience, as though you're dancing together.

- A unique buzz of togetherness and excitement is conjured that goes far beyond the sum of audience + speaker.
- You inspire courage in the room.
- Audiences remember and act upon what was said – hence, you have created change.

The challenge for an inspiring speaker is always to remain humble. Remember that it's *through you*, not *about you*, even if you are the one everyone is praising.

This place called inspiring speaking sounds both magical and terrifying. Instantly the negative self-talk comes in and says, 'Yes, but that's not for me – someone else would be much better.' This is exactly what this book has been about. You have the knowledge to connect with the audience and create a compelling talk. Now's the time to take the fearless leap into doing it.

Remember: public speaking is an act of leadership.

What if . . . I'm not a very inspiring person?

Expert tip: Caroline Goyder

'While it's true that some people naturally have bucket loads of charisma, and some don't, everyone can shine in front of an audience,' says Caroline Goyder,[38] author of *The Star Qualities*.[39] 'Think of all the actors and comedians who are shy off stage and switch it on in the spotlight. Cate Blanchett calls it "turning the lights on" and says she learned it at drama school.

'Turning the lights on is simple: you shine when you talk about someone you love, or something you are passionate about, or when you laugh. You focus your energy out on other people rather than into your worries or insecurities. It's the power of that generous feeling that gives you a glow and a sparkle. So, if you want to shine in front of an audience you have to make the audience feel something, and you do that by feeling something strongly yourself.

'To help this along, try George Clooney's trick of seeing the audience as old friends, so you relax, smile and sparkle. If all else fails, try the old actor's trick of having a naughty thought or a great secret – it works brilliantly for Johnny Depp!'

How to get fearless

1. Find your fight

I asked you in Chapter 1 to start your quest to find your personal purpose and beyond personal purpose for public speaking. Now's the time to return to that quest. As you look around your workplace and beyond, what needs someone to stick up for it? What do you care most about? And how can you fight for it in your public speaking? The fight might be explicit:

The fight . . .	Translates into a talk on . . .
Let's care more about people in the world	How we can nurture staff, customers and clients in this organisation
Let's stick up for freedom of speech	How we can stop the erosion of freedom of speech in the media
Let's be more mindful	Children would benefit from mindfulness practice – let's teach it in schools

Or if your inner purpose is very different to the subjects you're supposed to talk about, you can keep the fight more subtle:

The fight . . .	Translates into . . .
You're a marketing manager who wants to fight for human equality	Adding into your company overview presentation three stories: one from the CEO, one from a recent graduate who's just joined the company and one from a disabled employee in IT
You're an engineer who wants to fight for freedom	Making your presentations less rigid and more about freedom for your audience. Ask them questions, get them to move, take their suggestions – develop a speaking style that represents freedom, even if the topic is about something else
You're a politician who wants to fight for honesty above all things	Taking the decision to bring that honesty into all your public speaking encounters, no matter how tricky that may feel

As I mentioned before, if you have a big purpose it will bring power and fearlessness to your speaking – even if you are the only one who knows that purpose.

2. Remind yourself what you're fighting for

Once you've found your fight, it becomes a precious and important centre for all of your communications. If it really is the thing that you see as worth fighting for, it will help you to step into fearlessness when you're full of doubts. My fight is that in my work I'm sticking up for freedom and happiness.

Even I get lazy sometimes and find the nerves creeping back in. Sometimes I find myself saying, 'People aren't that interested in hearing you speak, don't bother putting your name forward. It's much more comfortable here at home.' Whenever I need to push through that mindset I remind myself: 'If you're *not* speaking, or you're *not* giving it the best you've got . . . just think of all the people who *aren't* benefiting.'

It's a sobering and maturing thought that frequently helps me to be fearless. After all, who am I to deny my audiences the benefit I can offer them?

3. Get strength from a guru

If you've ever been in a group waiting to bungee jump, you'll know that it's difficult to be the first person to take the plunge. We prefer to wait for someone else to check that it's safe. I keep saying that public speaking is an act of leadership and this is why: because it's us as inspiring speakers who need to take the first leap.

It can be helpful to remember that you're not the first speaker to ever do something scary. It helps to have an example of a speaker who has been bigger, bolder or more fearless than you. Watch them speak. Or read about their life. For me, Churchill is a constant inspiration – as a man who used the stubbornness of his convictions and the power of his voice to hold together a nation (and possibly an entire civilisation) at the time it was needed most. When I'm feeling shaky I remind myself to be solid and fearless like Churchill.

4. Visualise yourself fearless

Visualisation is a proven technique in building confidence and is used by sports people of all disciplines to help them hit their top performance on competition day. When you visualise, the same parts of the brain are stimulated as when you actually experience something, so it's likely that visualising success has a similar effect on confidence as actually experiencing success. In other words, visualising yourself as a fearless and inspiring speaker helps you to get there faster.

To allow a visualisation to work effectively, start with an open mind and try not to control or force where your mind takes you. A visualisation is a chance to switch off your logical mind and tap into your subconscious. Visualisations often work best if someone else guides you through, so that you can close your eyes and listen.

Alternatively, find a quiet space to read through the visualisation below, giving yourself plenty of time to sink into each stage of the process. It will take 10–20 minutes, so make sure you won't be interrupted. It's useful to keep a pen and paper handy, since the moment we relax thoughts can pop up that we don't want to forget. If that's the case, just write down 'Take dog for walk' so that you won't have to cling to the thought any more.

You can stand or sit during the visualisation, but standing is often better when you're visualising public speaking as it will help your body to rehearse its full power.

Confidence visualisation

1. Find a quiet space where you won't be disturbed. Close your eyes if you like and start to focus on your breath, letting any nerves or panicked thoughts just drift by.

2. As you focus on your breath, imagine you're breathing in a colour you associate with confidence and breathing out a colour you associate with negativity.

3. Spend 5–10 minutes using this method to get into a state of confidence and positivity. Let your body shape change as you feel more confident. Allow your shoulders to come back, your chest to open. Feel yourself growing in height. Keep breathing in confidence and breathing out negativity.

4. Now, glowing with confidence, imagine yourself stepping into the room or onto the stage that you are speaking from. If you know what the room is like, move yourself there slowly and confidently, noticing all the details you can on the way. If you can't imagine the room, just enjoy the sense that you're walking into a room that is filled with positive people.

5. Stand in front of your audience, taking a moment to enjoy the sensation of being the centre of attention. Notice that you're not daunted by the prospect of speaking. Feel confident, calm and supported by the audience. They can't wait to hear what you have to say and you can't wait to say it. Spend some time here, enjoying the moments before you start to speak. You may choose to look members of your audience in the eye, or to breathe in the atmosphere of the room. Do what it takes to get yourself feeling familiar and happy with your surroundings.

6. Now, as you start to speak, feel how it is to be in the body of a confident and fearless speaker. Allow yourself to move with confidence. You can even physically move as you visualise this. Enjoy the sensation of moving with power.

7. As you continue through your speech, you find yourself whisked into the minds of the audience. You are now watching yourself speaking. You are amazed at how confident, how knowledgeable and how entertaining you are as a speaker. Take a moment to watch what it is that you're doing as a speaker to show that confidence. Is it in the way

you walk? How you use your voice? How you interact with your audience?

8. As you start to wrap up what you have to say, you find your-self back in your own body. Your time in the public eye has gone better than you could have imagined. Look at all the grinning faces and smiling eyes in the audience. As you say your final words, allow your audience to thank you for what you had to say. Do they cheer? Has their perspective shifted profoundly? What impact have your fearless words had on your audience?

9. Soak up this feeling – this is your power as a speaker. It exists inside you, whether or not you've let it out so far.

10. Finally, take with you the feelings of calm and power that exist within your room and pull them inside a part of your body where your confidence lives. This is usually your heart or your stomach. Know that all that confidence is there for you to access whenever you need it. And with that, you can gently come back to your present state and open your eyes.

This is one suggestion that might work for you, but feel free to develop your own method of visualising. To benefit from the maximum impact, visualise your success daily in the run-up to your big talk.

5. Make a speaker's promise

Once you have a visual impression of who you'd like to be as a speaker, it can help to sharpen and hone that image into a speaker's promise you silently make every time you step on stage. It's a stage persona of sorts, but it's authentic rather than acted because it comes from your inner power and conviction.

Look for a set of qualities you wish to embody when you speak and then design a metaphor, set of words or image that reflects those qualities.

My speaker's promise is something like a Jack-in-the-box. The box is a reminder to stay grounded and to focus everything I say in a place of meaning. The spring represents the unique experience I promise to give every audience. And the stick person who comes out at the top is Ginger – the character who not only represents my company, Ginger Training & Coaching, but who symbolises energy, passion and childlike enthusiasm.

Each time I stand up to speak I remind myself of my speaker's promise, so that little by little, I step more into these qualities.

Your speaker's promise should be a challenge. Every time you look at it, it should encourage you to be a little bolder with your speaking. In time, you and your speaker's promise will become one and the same thing.

I've also seen people using special items of jewellery, a certain colour of clothing, or a particular piece of music to help them step into their fearless power. Do whatever works for you.

Part

At the centre of your being you have the answer;
you know who you are and you know what you want.

Lao Tzu

William Wobbletalk felt a lump in his throat. He hadn't realised his boss would be watching him talk. His stomach started churning.

'Oh no, she won't think I'm professional enough,' he found himself thinking. 'Maybe I should cut out the ice-breaker, or speed the discussion up a bit.' He fumbled with his PowerPoint clicker. 'Welcome to my projector,' he said, then blushed. 'Um, I mean, welcome to my presentation.' A few members of the audience folded their arms.

William took a deep breath, let the disturbance pass and started again. This time he was ready.

Authenticity

In Part 6:

- What happens when we lose authenticity.

- How to get grounded even if you're put off by something that happens while you're speaking.

We have come full circle back to authenticity. In this final part we'll investigate how to put authenticity into action.

Without the other five elements of the Public Speaking House, authenticity would be possible, but not powerful. Imagine a speaker who gushes from the heart, but in doing so uses dozens of 'ums', talks for far too long and forgets to say the things the audience wanted to hear. The audience may sympathise with them as a person, but their speaking will have limited power. Likewise, a speaker who is aware, empathetic, fresh, balanced and fearless can still lose their audience by coming across as false.

Authenticity is your chance to say powerfully, 'This is who I am, this is what I believe in and I will not budge from my message.' It enables you to engage with your audience, who will be persuaded to take on your message. Authenticity, then, is an important cherry on your public speaking cake.

However, in moments of panic, as with William Wobbletalk earlier, it's easy to lose confidence in yourself. Suddenly your relaxed, authentic self is nowhere to be seen.

Chapter

12

Key wisdom from this chapter

- **It doesn't matter if something goes wrong** . . . what matters is how you deal with it. Confident speakers return to their authentic state, rather than turning to a defensive mechanism.

- **Become a weeble:** every time something puts you off, learn to return to your centre by learning to access your inner confidence.

- **Get the right type of feedback:** look for feedback that affirms your authentic qualities rather than criticises your specific behaviours. When you feel relaxed, your behaviours will naturally be powerful anyway.

- **Unleash your extraordinary authentic power:** the most powerful version of you goes beyond 'habitual' authenticity to the real you that might never normally be seen. It's authentic because it feels true, but it takes you into a completely different league – that of an inspiring speaker.

- **Stretch into unchartered territory:** to find your extraordinary authentic power, look to contrasting characteristics to those you normally express. Our personalities are multi-dimensional, so the chances are you'll spot some new way of being that benefits your audience.

It ends with authenticity

How we lose our authenticity

You enter a speaking scenario with certain assumptions: assumptions of how you will behave, assumptions of how your audience will behave and assumptions of how your surroundings and equipment will behave. These assumptions prop up your ability to be your relaxed, confident self. When something goes wrong we become panicked and step into 'coping' behaviours that don't reflect our real, authentic selves. For example: 'I'm expecting 30 people, who I hope will be polite and well mannered. I have my speech prepared, I've timed it to exactly 10 minutes. My notes are in my back pocket just in case and I've practised using my props. What could possibly go wrong?'

This speaker's confidence is being propped up by the number of people in his audience, by their good manners, by his estimated timing, his back-up notes and his props.

Should a couple of his assumptions be bent, he may be able to adapt and retain his authenticity. For example, if only 15 people show up instead of the 30, he may be OK.

But if enough of these assumptions snap – meaning that the situation suddenly and dramatically changes – he may be thrown off-centre. Let's say the CEO unexpectedly comes to watch the talk, the speaker's just spilt water down his trousers and those notes that were safe in the back pocket have mysteriously disappeared. How do you stay cool even when you're in the thick of a public speaking nightmare?

If you're not careful, snapped assumptions will lead to panic and you'll find yourself snapping into a defence mechanism, such as elevating your status by pretending to be serious or important, waffling when you could just stay silent, or over-apologising.

None of these defence mechanisms is the authentic, relaxed you.

How to build authenticity

To express authenticity requires you to feel confident and stable in yourself. This is the state we know as being 'centred'. When you're centred, you have no need for worrying or second guessing because you are simply present in the moment, acting authentically and doing whatever is necessary.

From your calm centre, you start to discover how much power you have as a speaker.

In our earlier example, William Wobbletalk, an experienced speaker, loses his authenticity through making a mistake. Unfortunately this happens to speakers all the time. Authenticity is about learning how to remain in your centre, no matter what happens to put you off. In the excitement of preparing a talk, this 'inner' preparation is almost always forgotten.

I'll now share some techniques for staying centred, which will help you come back to your authentic state whenever you need it.

1. Manage your assumptions

Prepare yourself by noticing the assumptions that form the foundations of your success. These are the safety blankets that you rely on – so long as they are there, you feel balanced. Remove a safety blanket and you feel less able to perform.

What and who are you relying on to ensure you're successful? Are you secretly banking on:

- your audience being of a certain age (then I'll impress them)?
- a particular knowledge level (then my content will work)?
- a certain room layout (then I'll be able to do this exercise, which will make them enjoy the talk)?
- being able to use particular equipment (then I'll look good)?

Shine a light on all the safety blanket thoughts you might be whispering to yourself, such as: 'I'm fine so long as the audience aren't too knowledgeable', or 'I really hope my boss isn't there.'

Once you've noticed these assumptions, you have a choice:

1. Hold fast to your safety blankets and do everything you can to manipulate your external environment, so that you won't have to face something that puts you off-balance.

2. Learn how to become a weeble – one of those toy clowns with a rounded bottom. No matter how hard you push it, it will always come back to balance upright at its centre. A weeble adapts to changing circumstances without being thrown.

As long as you lay your foundations for success in conditions that you can't control, you're setting yourself up for a wobbly ride. Surprises are inevitable in public speaking, because you have an audience with a will of their own. So, rather than fighting a losing battle to control the uncontrollable, strengthen your calm core by laying your foundations for success in yourself.

2. Becoming a weeble

Step 1: Find your confidence within

Collect evidence that you will do a good job, no matter what happens. Find confidence in the following:

- Your experience in the subject matter. What knowledge or unique angle do you have that won't disappear, no matter how well the talk goes?

- Your ability to succeed. Think about all the times you've succeeded in something, whether it's public speaking or a related challenge from a different part of your life. Notice that even if things go wrong, at your core is someone who can – and does – succeed.

- How you shine when you're at your most comfortable. There's not a person in the world who isn't fun, interesting and inspirational when they're around their closest friends. This is the core of who you are, irrespective of what happens when you're speaking.

Step 2: Let disturbances pass

When we feel socially anxious, we tend to judge feedback we receive more harshly. Reduce the impact of unexpected circumstances by practising allowing them to pass without reacting. After all, there's no such thing as an objectively bad event, only your interpretation of it. As much as it might seem as though you have an evil laptop and projector that refuse to cooperate with you, the failure of your equipment is not objectively bad, it's you who can choose to make it so. If you allow your authentic self to act, you could choose to let the disturbance of the failed projector pass and see it as an opportunity to try something different with your audience.

Knowing that you should let disturbances pass is different to being able to do it. To train yourself, try mindfulness meditation, which has been shown to reduce stress and increase self-esteem. Mindfulness meditation means simply watching your thoughts come and go, without following them. You can practise it by:

- finding a quiet spot to sit for 10 minutes a day in the lead-up to your big talk
- aiming to sit and be present in the moment and to let any thoughts of past or future just go by
- not stopping, controlling or restricting thoughts – simply letting them pass without judging.

With patience and time, you will learn to distance yourself from disturbing thoughts so that you don't get knocked so far off course when difficulties arise. You can access your centred, weeble state in the middle of public speaking, simply by pausing and focusing on your breath.

Step 3: When you become derailed

But what if you can't just move on? Perhaps you've gone blank, or are blushing violently. What can you do to get back to your centre quickly? Here are some emergency methods:

1. **Take a sip of water:** this is normal behaviour for a speaker, so your audience will have no idea you've slipped up. A sip of water forces you to breathe and allows you to gain the space to step back into your centre.

2. **Change your posture:** notice how you tighten up when you lose your centre. This is your body's reaction to embarrassment. Become aware of that and shift your posture to how you stand when you're feeling completely at ease. The shift in posture gives the brain a signal to shift emotional state.

3. **Call for someone else's input:** if appropriate, ask the audience a question or a colleague to comment, to give yourself time to regroup.

4. **Laugh!** There's no audience in the world who want to see you struggle, so if everything goes wrong, just look on it with humour. This is often the most authentic reaction to a problem and it will help your audience see you as a real person.

Going beyond: the power of authenticity

The very best speakers are not those who have the biggest audiences or the grandest salaries. The best speakers are those who touch their audience on a profound level because of their ability to fully unleash their authenticity. These speakers are able to act in a way that's beyond personal. They forget themselves and their nagging worries as a speaker and completely focus on what the audience – and that moment – need. If you're truly authentic, you're able to access whatever state is needed because you know it's beneficial. You can risk the discomfort, or disagreement, of the audience in the service of the higher purpose.

Notice that authenticity isn't about expressing every emotion you happen to feel. 'Indulgent' authenticity risks damaging the empathy pillar. For example, telling your 'idiot' audience just how frustrated you are with them could damage the group dynamics. However, if used to benefit the audience, your frustration could be just the trigger needed to make a breakthrough in their learning or their willingness to change. If you are aware and empathetic, you will gain a sense of when to express yourself fully.

Habitual authentic power

As we mentioned in Part 1, so often public speakers are trained by being told what they're doing wrong. At one popular speaking club it's common to hear feedback like 'You said 12 ums, you stepped back and forth more than 7 times and you only made eye contact with 3 people. Otherwise it was good, well done.' People come to my workshops saying that feedback like that has left them traumatised!

The problem with this type of feedback is that while the speaker knows what she's doing wrong, she has no knowledge of her inspirational qualities, or how to access them. This will make her a shy or cautious speaker who is *avoiding being wrong*, rather than an authentic speaker who is allowing her personality and heart to show.

When my Ginger team and I give feedback to speakers we're always looking for the *habitual authentic power* of a speaker, or the qualities that they display that are already inspiring. That might be one speaker's enthusiasm, another's humour and someone else's gravitas. We focus on these qualities, not to praise them per se but to point out where their authentic power naturally lies and help them feel safe within it. Feedback using this method would sound more like, 'Wow, do you know that you have a really grounded style? You're very solid in your feet. What we need now is for your gestures to be a touch more intentional, then you will seem very trustworthy as a speaker.'

When you are relaxed and authentic, your behaviours, like those ums and gestures, naturally become more powerful anyway.

Extraordinary authentic power

Full authenticity means using all of your personality or showing us the parts of your personality that you usually reserve for particular people or situations. This kind of expression is still *you*, so it's still authentic, but it might feel unusual or uncomfortable to let it be part of your speaking.

It's difficult to spot your extraordinary authentic power without feedback as it could be a part of you that you've carefully learned to hide. James, for example, is a brilliant young stand-up comic who came to me to explore his public speaking. Humour was of course always there in his speaking – and many other qualities, too. But when my co-trainer Rona pointed out to him the depth and silence she intuitively felt him to have, his speaking took on a completely new level. This new place of silence and depth was part of James, he recognised, but it hadn't been let out before. In this way he acquired power that was both authentic and extraordinary.

To develop your *extraordinary authentic power,* look for a contrast in style that will complement your habitual authentic power.

Try a new style

Notice more your habitual style as a speaker. Do you always tell a joke? Do you jump straight into the details? Are you the 'excited' speaker? Are you comfortable only when you're in dialogue with your audience?

Choose a contrasting part of your personality to bring into your speaking when you need to influence or inspire (often when you're reaching the climax in your hero's journey). Because it is less practised than other parts of your on-stage persona, it may come out in a way that's raw, emotional or messy. Whatever the outcome, embrace it! So long as it's authentic, your audience will welcome it, too.

These are some style contrasts that work well together:

- **Informer vs storyteller:** if you're a speaker who uses a lot of information or a very persuasive message, balance that power by switching into a mode that's personal, human and focused on stories. Although it may feel uncomfortable to lose some of your evidence, what you'll gain is greater connection to your audience.

- **Humour vs sincerity:** perhaps you've just delivered an entertaining wedding speech. You have your audience rolling in the aisles. You could leave it at that, or you could pause for a second and say, 'But in all seriousness, I love this woman.' Switching to a sincere or even serious moment after you've had the audience laughing will bring them powerfully down to earth in a way that they'll remember. This is how classic comedies such as *Cold Feet* and *Scrubs* manage to create their most heart-wrenching moments.

- **Energy vs calm:** everyone loves an energetic presenter, but if you're at the same energy level for your whole talk, you're missing an opportunity to impact your audience. Create balance by putting some moments of calm into your talk. This could be physical stillness as well as speaking in a calmer fashion. This contrast will further emphasise the power of your energy, while giving it a few moments to sink in. Likewise, if you're a typically calm presenter, challenge yourself to inject a burst of energy to show the audience key moments of passion or enthusiasm.

- **Got-it-sorted vs messy:** speakers who are super polished are great, but sometimes we can't relate to them. Their talks can feel just a little too planned. If this sounds like you, give yourself permission to 'go messy'. Embrace mistakes, laugh at yourself, spontaneously try a story you haven't told before. The results will completely shift the energy in the room.

- **Mr Nice Guy vs Mrs Hard Nose:** if you regularly seek affirmation from your audience, or look to create consensus in the room, you could be a Mr Nice Guy speaker. Don't get caught up in the need to be liked by everyone in your audience. This will make you mild, but not inspirational. Balance your Mr Nice Guy, which will win you friends in the audience, with Mrs Hard Nose. These are moments of 'telling it how it is' where you don't apologise, edit or moderate what you're saying:

  - Mrs Hard Nose: 'This is bad.'
  - Mr Nice Guy: 'Sorry to say, but it's not really all that good, I don't think.' This style switch, used wisely, will call your audience to action. They will like and respect you even more as a result.

This style switch, used wisely, will call your audience to action. They will like and respect you even more as a result.

To switch your style takes courage as you're often breaking the rapport you have worked so hard to build. Rapport is useful only if you use it to create an impact. If you avoid breaking rapport, you are pulling away from your full power as a speaker.

The great majority of public speakers-in-waiting pull away from their power because they're unaware they can move an audience. 'Who am I to make people laugh and cry?' 'Who am I to be a catalyst?' 'Who am I to be a speaker who changes people's lives?' As Marianne Williamson said,[40] 'Who are you not to be?'

In fact, all you have to do is not actually 'do' anything, it's to *be*. It's to be authentic.

The road ahead

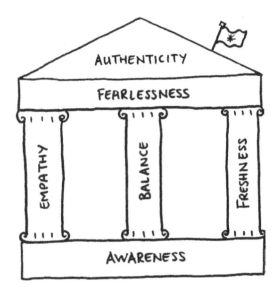

You have everything you need to become a brilliant public speaker. Now you just need to go out and practise. After all, it's difficult to be a better public speaker if you don't practise public speaking.

Ways to practise include:

- visiting a local speaking club such as Toastmasters (although be sure to look for affirming feedback that strengthens your inspirational qualities, rather than a list of how many 'ums' you said during your talk)
- actively seeking opportunities to speak through your work-place – just say yes rather than needing to be right first time

- joining one of my public speaking courses through my company Ginger Training & Coaching
- or, if all else fails, video yourself speaking and getting someone to give you feedback – even a virtual audience will help you overcome your nerves.

The six qualities of an inspiring speaker

As you practise, remember to strengthen each of the six qualities of an inspiring speaker. Here are the key words of wisdom from each:

- **Authenticity: you inspire by being yourself.** By connecting with a beyond personal purpose that's meaningful for you, your public speaking takes on authentic great power.
- **Awareness: choose to avoid falling down the hole.** Get curious about what is going on with your body, your voice and your nerves. Choose to pick up the powerful behaviours and drop the weird stuff.
- **Empathy: becoming a servant speaker.** There's one of you – and many of them: who does it make most sense to focus on? Stop obsessing about yourself and focus on your audience.
- **Balance: take your audience on a hero's journey.** Focus your talk on one powerful *idea worth spreading*. Take your audience to the summit of a mountain, then airlift them home.
- **Freshness: do something your audience will remember for ever.** Have the courage to be memorable. Use all the creative tools at your disposal to create an experience for your audience: visuals, verbal devices and interactive tools.
- **Fearlessness: public speaking is an act of leadership.** Channel the energy of nerves into excitement that benefits your audience. Push beyond your habitual comfort zone to new territories that add colour and power to your speaking.

And remember, you *can* inspire by being yourself – in fact, that's the only way it's going to happen.

Further resources

I've put together a website with a wealth of resources to support you on your public speaking journey. Head over to www.gingerpublicspeaking.com for the following:

- **Free public speaking e-course:** your free public speaking email coaching based around the 'ginger doodle' illustrations in this book. You'll receive a series of beautiful doodles and public speaking tips over six weeks.

- **Featured talks:** videos and commentary on famous talks I have mentioned in this book.

- **Online workshops:** to help you overcome public speaking fear and strengthen all parts of your performance – recommended if you want to take the lessons from this book further.

- **Upcoming in-person workshops from Ginger Training & Coaching:** open to all aspiring speakers. If you're serious about becoming a brilliant speaker, these are not to be missed.

- **Videos from our six-month Inspiring Speakers Programme graduates.** A selection of short talks from speakers who have been fully trained on the six qualities of an inspiring speaker. Many of them started from zero public speaking confidence, so do take a look. It's incredible what can happen when you decide to inspire.

You can also find me on Twitter@gingernibbles and Facebook at www.facebook.com/goginger.

What did you think of this book?

We're really keen to hear from you about this book, so that we can make our publishing even better.

Please log on to the following website and leave us your feedback.

It will only take a few minutes and your thoughts are invaluable to us.

www.pearsoned.co.uk/bookfeedback

References

[1] From a speech she gave in London, for the School of Life, Conway Hall, 3 July 2013.

[2] McCroskey, James C. (2009) 'Communication Apprehension: What have we learned in the last four decades?', *Human Communication: A Journal of the Pacific and Asian Communication Association,* 12(2), pp. 157–171 (available at www.uab.edu/Communicationstudies/humancommunication/merge.pdf).

[3] Steptoe, A. (2001) 'Negative emotions in music making: The problem of performance anxiety', in Juslin, P.N. and Sloboda, J.A. (eds.) *Music and Emotion: Theory and research,* Oxford: Oxford University Press, pp. 291–307.

[4] Bruskin Associates (1973) 'What are Americans afraid of?', *The Bruskin Report,* p. 53. This survey isn't publicly accessible, but was reported in a *Sunday Times* article entitled, 'What people usually fear', 7 October 1973, p. 9.

[5] Available at www.communicationcache.com/uploads/1/0/8/8/10887248/patterns_of_psychological_state_anxiety_in_public_speaking_as_a_function_of_anxiety_sensitivity.pdf

[6] See, for example, Van Raalte, J.L., Brewer, B.W., Lewis, B.P. and Linder, D.E. (1995) 'Cork! The effects of positive and negative self-talk on dart throwing performance', *Journal of Sport Behavior,* 18(1), p. 50.

[7] Clark, D.M. and Wells, A. (1995) 'A cognitive model of social phobia', in Heimberg, R.R.G, Liebowitz, M., Hope, D.A. and Scheier S. (eds.) *Social Phobia: Diagnosis, assessment and treatment,* New York: Guilford.

[8] Frost, R.O. and Marten, P.A. (1990) 'Perfectionism and evaluative threat', *Cognitive Therapy and Research,* 14(6), pp. 559–572.

[9] Conroy, D.E., Willow, J.P. and Metzler, J.N. (2002) 'Multidimensional fear of failure measurement: The Performance Failure Appraisal Inventory', *Journal of Applied Sport Psychology,* 14(2), pp. 76–90.

[10] Wells, A., Clark, D.M. and Ahmad, S. (1998) 'How do I look with my mind's eye: Perspective taking in social phobic imagery', *Behaviour Research and Therapy,* 36(6), pp. 631–634.

[11] In an interview with the author.

[12] Andersen, J.F. (1979) 'Teacher immediacy as a predictor of teaching effectiveness', in Nimmo, D. (ed.), *Communication Yearbook 3,* New Brunswick, NJ: Transaction Books, pp. 543–559.

REFERENCES

[13] Erk, S., Kiefer, M., Grothe, J., Wunderlich, A.P., Spitzer, M. and Walter, H. (2003) 'Emotional context modulates subsequent memory effect', *NeuroImage*, 18(2), pp. 439–447.

[14] Risner, N. (2002) *It's a Zoo Around Here: The new rules for better communication*, Lydbrook: Forest Oak.

[15] In an interview with the author.

[16] Mann, R.D., Arnold S., Binder, J., Cytrynbaum S., Newman, B.M., Ringwald, B., Ringwald, J. and Rosenwein, R. (1970) *The College Classroom: Conflict, change and learning*, New York: John Wiley.

[17] In an interview with the author.

[18] In an interview with the author.

[19] Mehrabian, A. (1971) *Silent Messages: Implicit communication of emotions and attitudes*, Belmont, CA: Wadsworth.

[20] Booher, D. (2003) *Speak with Confidence: Powerful presentations that inform, inspire, and persuade*, New York and London: McGraw-Hill.

[21] Available at www.ted.com/talks/brian_goldman_doctors_make_mistakes_can_we_talk_about_that

[22] Campbell, J. (1972) [1949] *The Hero with a Thousand Faces* (2nd ed.), Princeton, NJ: Princeton University Press.

[23] Available at www.youtube.com/watch?v=J5gp_1cGuZo

[24] In an interview with the author.

[25] Recorded at a Moshé Feldenkrais workshop, Rotterdam, November 1976.

[26] In an interview with the author.

[27] In an interview with the author.

[28] Thagard, P. (2005) 'How to be a successful scientist', in Gorman, M.E., Tweney, R.D., Gooding, D.C. and Kincannon, A.P. (eds.) *Scientific and Technological Thinking*, Mawah, NJ: Lawrence Erlbaum Associates, pp. 159–171.

[29] In an interview with the author.

[30] Available at www.ted.com/talks/ken_robinson_says_schools_kill_creativity?language=en#t-42160

[31] In an interview with the author.

[32] See www.ted.com/speakers/simon_sinek

[33] See www.ted.com/speakers/hans_rosling

[34] In an interview with the author.

[35] See www.ted.com/speakers/sir_ken_robinson

[36] See www.ted.com/talks/jamie_oliver

[37] Atkinson, C. (2010) *The Backchannel: How audiences are using Twitter and social media and changing presentations forever*, Berkeley, CA: New Riders.

[38] In an interview with the author.

[39] Goyder, C. (2009) *The Star Qualities: How to sparkle with confidence in all aspects of your life*, London: Sidgwick & Jackson.

[40] Williamson, M. (1992) *A Return to Love: Reflections on the principles of 'A Course in Miracles'*, New York: HarperCollins.

Index

Do you want your people to be the very best at what they do?

Talk to us about how we can help.

As the world's leading learning company, we know a lot about what your people need in order to be better at what they do.

Whatever subject or skills you've got in mind (from presenting or persuasion to coaching or communication skills), and at whatever level (from new-starters through to top executives) we can help you deliver tried-and-tested, essential learning straight to your workforce – whatever they need, whenever they need it and wherever they are.

Talk to us today about how we can:

- Complement and support your existing learning and development programmes
- Enhance and augment your people's learning experience
- Match your needs to the best of our content
- Customise, brand and change it to make a better fit
- Deliver cost-effective, great value learning content that's proven to work.

Contact us today:
corporate.enquiries@pearson.com

ALWAYS LEARNING

PEARSON